Charles d'Orléans

Twayne's World Authors Series

Maxwell Smith, Editor
Guerry Professor of French, Emeritus
The University of Chattanooga
Former Visiting Professor in Modern Languages
The Florida State University

TWAS 699

Calendar scene of April from the *Très Riches Heures* of the Duke of Berry.
Photograph by Photographie Giraudon.
Reproduced courtesy of Musée Condé, Chantilly.

Charles d'Orléans

By David A. Fein

University of North Carolina at Greensboro

Twayne Publishers • *Boston*

Charles d'Orléans

David A. Fein

Copyright © 1983 by G.K. Hall & Company
All Rights Reserved
Published by Twayne Publishers
A Division of G. K. Hall & Company
70 Lincoln Street
Boston, Massachusetts 02111

Printed on permanent/durable acid-free
paper and bound in the United States of
America.

Library of Congress Cataloging in Publication Data

Fein, David A.
    Charles d'Orléans.

    (Twayne's world author series; TWAS 699)
    Bibliography: p.161
    Includes index.
    1. d'Orléans, Charles, 1394–1465—Criticism
and interpretation. I. Title. II. Series.
PQ1553.C5F44   1983   841'.2   83-5838
ISBN 0-8057-6546-8

For my parents
and for Rita

Contents

About the Author

Preface

Chronology

CHAPTER ONE
Introduction   1

CHAPTER TWO
Biographical Sketch   13

CHAPTER THREE
The Early Ballad Cycle   23

CHAPTER FOUR
The Complainte to France   54

CHAPTER FIVE
The Narrative Poems   63

CHAPTER SIX
The Songs   75

CHAPTER SEVEN
The English Poetry   84

CHAPTER EIGHT
Prince of the Poetic Court   88

CHAPTER NINE
The Later Ballads   96

CHAPTER TEN
The Rondeaux   115

CHAPTER ELEVEN
Conclusion   146

Notes and References   155

Selected Bibliography   161

Index   164

About the Author

David A. Fein received the B.A. from Brown University in 1971 and the Ph.D. from Cornell University in 1976. He has also studied at the Centre de Philologie in Strasbourg. Since 1976 he has taught French at the University of North Carolina at Greensboro where he currently holds the rank of associate professor. His articles on medieval French lyric poetry have appeared in Romance Philology, Fifteenth-Century Studies, Neophilologus, Neuphilologische Mitteilungen, and Medioevo Romanzo. He is presently completing a monograph on François Villon. Professor Fein is a member of Phi Beta Kappa.

Preface

Charles d'Orléans, long neglected and underrated as a poet, is finally beginning to emerge from the shadow of François Villon. The present reappraisal of his work may be explained partly by a recently revived interest in medieval poetics, as well as by the attention he has received from such highly respected medievalists as Daniel Poirion and Paul Zumthor. Within the last fifteen years four important books have been devoted to his work, the most recent and ambitious of which is the lengthy study by Alice Planche.

Despite this increase of critical interest, Charles d'Orléans remains relatively unknown or misknown by American students of French literature. Editors of anthologies tend to dismiss his poetry as well crafted but uninspired. The author of one introductory survey of French literature widely used in American universities describes the poet's work as characterized "by dainty but not vigorous fancy." This condescension merely perpetuates the nineteenth-century prejudices that still plague Charles's reputation.

The purpose of the present study is to introduce Charles d'Orléans to those who are unfamiliar with his poetry and also possibly unacquainted with the vast body of French verse composed prior to the sixteenth century. With this audience in mind, I have included in my introduction a very brief summary of the literary and historical background of fifteenth-century French poetry. Unlike the authors of some previous studies of Charles d'Orléans, I have elected a generic rather than a thematic approach. This decision was based on a conviction that each genre represents a unique aspect of Charles's poetic personality and therefore warrants separate treatment. At the same time, I fully recognize the validity of a thematic approach for purposes other than those of this book. I have attempted insofar as possible to arrange my chapters in roughly chronological sequence in order to trace the basic lines of the poet's development. However, the lack of a reliable chronology and the chronological overlap of some genres make it impossible to study his poems in the precise order in which they were written.

Instead of examining the ballads as a homogeneous body, I have divided them according to whether they were written before or after Charles's repatriation in 1440. I believe this division to be justified by the numerous differences that distinguish the later ballad cycle from the earlier one. Rather than devote a chapter to the complaintes, I have selected the two most important for discussion in separate chapters. One, the Songe en complainte, is paired with an earlier allegorical narrative of which it is the sequel. The other, a fervently patriotic poem, holds a unique position in Charles's poetic corpus. The remaining complaintes duplicate themes and styles found in his other poetry and have therefore been omitted to avoid redundancy. The carols, also few in number, have been omitted for the same reason.

The most problematic question to arise during the organization of this study was how to deal with the manuscript of English verse that some scholars attribute to Charles d'Orléans. Critical opinion is sharply divided on the issue and does not appear to be moving toward any consensus. My solution was simply to summarize the evidence supporting each side of the dispute and evaluate the validity of each argument. To those who would take me to task for not giving more attention to this body of verse, I would cite its conspicuous absence in the study of Charles d'Orléans by John Fox, one of the strongest advocates of Charles's authorship. Until the source of the poems has been conclusively identified, it would seem presumptuous if not irresponsible to pass final judgment on the matter. The English poems have therefore been relegated to a peripheral position in the present study.

I have included a generous number of quotations from Charles d'Orléans's poetry in order to give the reader an adequate basis for forming judgments independent of my own. All citations are from Pierre Champion's edition, which since its publication in 1927 has been universally acknowledged as the most reliable published version of Charles's poetry. I confess I do not accept all of Champion's punctuation and capitalization (when used to indicate personification), but I have followed his textual interpretations, voicing personal

Preface

reservations only where I feel his reading to be misleading.

All translations of Charles's verse are my own. It is my hope that those readers who know French will use the translations only as a reference for difficult constructions and unknown words. Those who do not read French should be cautioned that no translation can do justice to the musical quality which is a vital aspect of all poetry.

I would like to acknowledge the helpful financial assistance provided toward the completion of this book by the University of North Carolina at Greensboro. To Professor Wallace Fowlie I am deeply grateful for suggesting the idea of this study and for encouraging me to pursue it. I also wish to thank Professors Alice Colby-Hall and Marcel Tetel for their endorsement of my proposal. I am indebted to my editor, Professor Maxwell A. Smith, for his patience, advice, and supportive communication. My colleague, Professor James C. Atkinson, with his usual cheerfulness and generosity donated a good deal of time and wisdom toward improving my manuscript. My father, Professor John M. Fein, also contributed numerous constructive remarks. I am grateful to him not only for the care with which he read my manuscript, but also for sharing with me, as long as I can remember, his extraordinary love of literature. Finally, I thank my wife, Rita, whose support has always been for me a source of confidence and inspiration.

David A. Fein

University of North Carolina at Greensboro

Chronology

1394   November 24: Charles born to Louis, Duke of Orléans and brother of King Charles VI, and Valentina, daughter of Duke of Milan.

1406   Marries Isabelle, widow of Richard II of England, daughter of Charles VI.

1407   Louis murdered by the hired assassins of Jean-sans-Peur.

1408   Valentina dies at Blois.

1409   Isabelle dies in childbirth.

1410   Marries Bonne d'Armagnac. Alliance signed between houses of Orléans and Armagnac.

1415   Battle of Azincourt. French suffer disastrous defeat; Charles taken prisoner, sent to England to be held for ransom.

1421   Sent to Fotheringhay (Northampton) to be kept in custody of Sir Thomas Burton.

1422   Transferred to Bolingbroke (Lincolnshire) under care of Sir Thomas Cunkerworth.

1430   Moved to Ampthill (Bedfordshire) in care of Sir John Cornwall.

1431   Jeanne d'Arc burned at the stake. Birth of Villon.

1431-1435   Learns of Bonne's death (year unknown).

1432   Transferred to Wingfield (Suffolk) in keeping of William de la Pole, Earl of Suffolk; close friendship develops between the two men. Makes acquaintance of Alice Chaucer, Suffolk's wife and Geoffrey Chaucer's granddaughter.

1433 Spends six weeks at Dover waiting for French delegation to peace conference.

1436 Moved to Sterborough (Surrey) in care of Sir Reynold Cobham.

1439 Taken to Calais to participate in treaty negotiations.

1440 Released from England thanks to intervention of his cousin, Philippe of Burgundy, and Phillipe's wife, Isabelle. Marries fourteen-year-old Marie de Clèves, Philippe's niece.

1444 Participates in signing of Treaty of Tours. His younger brother John is released from England after thirty-one years of imprisonment.

1447 Heads a military expedition to Italy in an effort to reclaim Asti.

1448 Returns to France to seek assistance.

1449 Travels to Lyon attempting to raise funds for a second expedition.

1450 Renounces attempt to reclaim Asti; retires to Blois.

1458 Treason trial of son-in-law, Duke of Alençon; delivers speech in Alençon's defense. Birth of daughter, Marie.

1462 Birth of first and only son, Louis, to become King Louis XII.

1465 January 4: death of Charles d'Orléans at Amboise.

Chapter One
Introduction

The achievement of a modern poet may generally be evaluated with minimal reference to the entire scope of poetic history underlying his particular contribution. To appreciate the importance of Rimbaud, for example, one need not view his poetry against the backdrop of ten centuries of French verse. Such is not the case for the medieval poet. The literary background which might be considered superfluous for Rimbaud becomes essential for a serious study of Charles d'Orléans or any of his contemporaries. However skilled the medieval poet, his unique talent was forced to operate within numerous constraints of form, language, and theme dictated by poetic tradition. Even François Villon, the poet most resistant to conformity, drew enormously upon the rich courtly heritage of which all late medieval poets were the beneficiaries. Given its profound effect on fifteenth-century French poetry, a brief review of this tradition may prove useful.

Origins of the Lyric

The known history of courtly poetry and the ideal it embodies begins in the second half of the eleventh century in the southeastern region of modern France. Here we find the first evidence of a somewhat mysterious process of cultural refinement that gradually tempered the war-oriented values of the feudal nobility. Outward manifestations of this refinement include the expansion of domestic staffs, the ostentatious display of wealth (particularly in the form of clothing), and architectural modifications designed to make castles more comfortable and a little less fortress-like. The purely functional was beginning to yield to the aesthetically pleasing. With this new cultural sophistication came the simultaneous elevation of the woman's role in noble society.

The increased respect and admiration accorded to women, an attitude expressed in terms formerly reserved

1

for the description of feudal relationships, form the
basis of courtoisie, or fin'amors as it was called
at the time (1). In courtly ideology the woman becomes
the lover's sovereign, his dame, and he, her vassal.
Their relationship is described by a curious amalgama-
tion of military, erotic, and religious language. To
what extent the condition of aristocratic women was
actually enhanced by their newly idealized status is
debatable. What we can say with certainty is that the
courtly myth exercised a very powerful and long-lived
influence on the medieval imagination. As one of the
several hypotheses that may be offered to explain the
rapid growth of this phenomenon, one may cite the useful psychological function served by the concept of
courtoisie. If feudalism allowed a man to define himself in relation to his society, and religion offered
him a channel for spiritual growth, in fin'amors he
found a way to order the troubling emotions of love,
desire, jealousy, and fear of rejection.

The deepest origins of the poetry celebrating
fin'amors remain obscure, having successfully eluded
generations of curious and imaginative scholars. Several major theories have been set forth, and each in
turn has stimulated vigorous debate. It has been suggested, for example, that the true sources of this
poetry lie in the Hispano-Arabic culture of the eleventh century. Another viewpoint considers the literary
movement an indigenous product whose roots may be found
in the folklore of southern France, especially in the
joyful dance songs commemorating the return of spring.
Still another hypothesis, and one which has stirred
considerable controversy, attempts to trace the genre
to religious origins, citing resemblances between litur-
gical praise of the Virgin and the love songs of the
troubadours. The fact remains that a conclusive identification of the real source or sources has yet to be
made.

The first recorded appearance of fin'amors is
found in the songs of the earliest troubadours:
Guillaume IX d'Aquitaine, Jaufré Rudel, Bernart de
Ventadorn, all of whom were highly skilled musicians as
well as talented poets (2). Their pieces, composed
prior to the end of the twelfth century, were written
in langue d'oc, a collection of dialects spoken in
southern France throughout the Middle Ages, sometimes
inaccurately grouped under the rubric of Provençal.

When referring to these earliest lyric specimens as poetry, it is important to bear in mind that we are actually speaking of songs, for these pieces were always performed as such, with or without instrumental accompaniment. (The word lyric, etymologically related to lyre, originally designated any poem suitable for singing to the accompaniment of this instrument.) The importance of the musical origins of French poetry cannot be overstated. Although the written text had clearly superseded song as the dominant lyric mode before the end of the fourteenth century, French verse remained marked by its troubadour sources throughout the remainder of the medieval period. The echo of the lyre is especially pervasive in the work of Charles d'Orléans who, although not a professional musician, possessed a remarkably sensitive ear for the melodious qualities of spoken verse.

From its inception and throughout most if its later development, medieval lyric verse maintained close ties with the aristocratic courts. In Aquitaine, Poitou, and Provence the massive châteaux, bastions of culture as well as military power, served as focal points for the new artistic movement. Whether the songs were performed by a member of the nobility, a minstrel attached to the court, or an itinerant poet, they were always directed to an aristocratic public. Not surprisingly, the aesthetic that developed in response to this restricted and privileged audience dictated an esoteric and highly refined form of art. Our modern sensibilities, unattuned to the subtleties of medieval poetics, may quickly tire of what appears to be the endless repetition of a handful of themes and images. But restored to its original musical form, and performed for ears sensitive to the slightest gradations of sound and meaning, each poem would convey a rich diversity of nuances.

Entertainment was only one function of the troubadour's song. More important was the poet's intention to uplift his audience, allowing it to enter with him into one of the less accessible realms of human existence. For these songs were mostly hymns of love, canzos d'amors, and true love was considered unattainable to all but a select few. Medieval love poetry was to carry this imprint of mystery and elitism throughout the course of its subsequent development.

As mentioned, the male-female relationship in the

canzo d'amors, an element which remained intact when
the song was later imported into northern France, is
based on a transposition of the vassal-lord relationship. The poet is bound to his lady, as is the vassal
to his lord, by unconditional loyalty. His fate is
entirely entrusted into her hands. A kind word from
her, a smile, a kiss, and the poet is immediately trans-
ported into a state of ecstasy. A sign of displeasure,
a hint of rejection, and he sinks into an abyss of despair. More than a sovereign, the woman takes on a kind
of divine authority over the man, and this apotheosis
is often reflected by the deliberate use of religiously
colored language.

The second characteristic of the love song is its
emphasis on the poet's suffering. Introspectively ori-
ented, the focus of the poem becomes not the woman or
the potential for happiness which she offers, but her
absence, and the negative feelings that this absence
generates in the poet's heart. Joy and fulfillment are
elusive. It is anguish, sorrow, loneliness, and longing that more often dominate the tone: "Alas, I
thought I knew so much of love, and I know of it so little! For I cannot help loving her from whom good will
never come to me. She has taken from me my heart, and
taken myself from me, and taken herself and all the
world; and when from me she took herself, she left me
naught but desire and a longing heart" (3). The suffering expressed in the canzo d'amors should not be
regarded, however, as a debasing experience. It proves
instead to be an elevating force tending toward purification rather than humiliation. The poet claims to sacrifice his health, his sanity, even his very life, all
for the cause of martyrdom. The theme of joi runs
contrapuntally through troubadour poetry, but it occurs
more frequently as the hope for success rather than the
contentment of possession.

The double theme of joy/anguish is only one of a
series of binary oppositions that characterize the canzo d'amors. The archetypal model for these dichoto-
mies is the opposition of light and darkness, which
gives rise to such antithetical pairs as: warmth/cold,
spring/winter, hope/despair, pleasure/pain, health/sick-
ness, union/solitude, freedom/imprisonment. Although
the "dark" side of the pair often tends to dominate,
the presence of the other half is always sensed. Winter will eventually make way for spring; solitude,

sickness, and pain may always be replaced by their positive counterparts. This poetry is pervaded by a constant temsion between the two poles of the psyche. The poet wavers between joy and despair, always keeping his precarious balance with the element of hope.

By the early thirteenth century the influence of the troubadours was evident in a number of European literatures including those of Germany, Portugal, Italy, and northern France. The imported canzo d'amors thrived in the provinces of Champagne, Lorraine, and Picardy where it was reworked in the French dialects by the trouvères: Gace Brulé, Conon de Béthune, Thibaut de Champagne, Adam de la Halle, to cite a few of the most popular. While the language changed, the chanson d'amour remained remarkably close to its southern prototype in style, tone, and theme. But the fourteenth century, a period of social, political, and economic upheaval in France, would bring about significant changes in this long-static form of art.

Historical Background of Later Medieval Poetry

Three historical phenomena affected fourteenth- and early fifteenth-century French society, and consequently most literary forms of the period. The first of these was the Hundred Years' War, the name given to the series of hostilities between the English and the French that erupted intermittently from 1337 to 1453. The material damage inflicted by invading troops was far less significant than the impact of the protracted struggle on the spirit of the French. Of course, all social classes, as in any war, were subjected to various degrees of physical hardship. But the hardest blow, for the nobility at least, was the loss of traditional values. One of the by-products of the long conflict was a sense of disillusionment, and a simultaneous nostalgia for the chivalric ideals that had suffered so grievously under the strain of this "modern" war. Traditional warfare had pitted opponents against each other in personal combat. The merits of such battle and its potential for inspiring acts of honor and heroism are warmly praised in the Chanson de Roland and other early French epics. But the Hundred Years' War represented an innovation in warfare. The English, far outnumbered by their adversaries and fighting at a disadvantage in enemy territory, resourcefully resorted

to the extensive use of highly trained archers and to
skillful military maneuvering. Their tactics met with
tremendous success. Encumbered by their unwieldy armor
and unaccustomed to this more impersonal style of combat, the French suffered disastrous defeats at the
hands of smaller English armies at Crécy (1346),
Poitiers (1356), and Azincourt (1415). Besides depriv-
ing France of the flower of her nobility, these routs
dealt crippling blows to the morale of the aristocracy.

The fourteenth-century chronicler and poet Jean
Froissart tried in his chronicles to restore to the war
the chivalric aura it had so quickly lost. But an
attentive reading of his narration reveals cracks in
the veneer of respectability that he attempts to paint
over the conflict. What Froissart's futile effort demonstrates most is a painful awareness of the deterioration of the feudal order with its chivalric code and
outmoded ideals. Many of the noblemen whose fathers
and grandfathers would have been welcomed into Roland's
valiant army found themselves leading bands of rou-
tiers, unemployed soldiers and foreign mercenaries who
marauded through the countryside, murdering, raping,
and pillaging during periods of "peace."

The evolution of warfare toward depersonalization of
combat, the decline of the feudal order and its traditional values, and a growing apprehension of the threat
posed by the rising bourgeoisie, all combined to test
severely the morale of the nobility. In addition to
the humanly generated crisis of war, Frenchmen of every
social class faced a natural disaster whose effects
were even more widespread, the bubonic plague. Brought
from the Crimea, the disease first penetrated Europe
via Genoa in 1347. By the middle of the following year
the plague was raging through France, and by 1350 hardly a family on the Continent or in England remained
untouched. The Black Death, so called for the dusky
color with which it left its victims, was characterized
by fever, chills, hemorrhages beneath the skin, swelling of the lymph nodes in the groin and armpits, and
intense pain. In the wake of its first sweep through
Europe and during the course of several successive
waves throughout the remainder of the century, it left
dead at least a third of the total population (4).

The plague stained not only the skin of its victims,
but also the minds of the survivors. The event was
widely accepted by theologians and laity alike as a

divine retribution for a collective state of sin. Here for all to see was the most vivid illustration one could possibly imagine of man's weakness and mortality. The somber themes of human frailty, suffering, and death became increasingly popular as the focus for meditations, sermons, and poetry. The motif of the danse macabre begins to appear in art and literature. A string of dancers representing every social condition from pope to pauper is led here by the figure of death, allegorically portrayed as a wildly grinning skeleton. One need not look far to discover the grim side of this age. Indeed it can scarcely be avoided. Images of deterioration, torment, and death are everywhere.

The portrait of late medieval French society should not, however, be painted only in dark colors. In spite of the formidable obstacles it had to surmount, the French economy proved remarkably resilient. While the feudal order was dying and the aristocracy was losing ground (in every sense), commerce was prospering as never before. The rapid growth of commercial enterprise and the subsequent proliferation of the legal profession produced a dynamic new social class. By the end of the fourteenth century the bourgeoisie was firmly rooted in France. Although less powerful than the Italian borghese, the French bourgeois was nonetheless a political force not to be treated lightly, as the nobility painfully learned on numerous occasions (5).

With the gradual shift of political power from a feudal to a commercial base, the aristocracy found its privileges being insidiously undermined by the power of money. The once impenetrable barrier separating the noble and the non-noble was breaking down. Chiefly through the acquisition of land, families of modest lineage but considerable wealth and ambition were able eventually to acquire coats of arms and legal recognition of nobility. The social and economic conditions of the period were ideal for stimulating an intense hunger for power and prestige. This greed for social status manifested itself in a number of ways, but most strikingly in the conspicuous exhibition of material wealth. Pretentious houses, tapestries, banquets, and showy clothes, all formerly prerogatives of the aristocracy, were now appropriated by the bourgeoisie. Since the criteria for establishing social supremacy were no longer hard and fast, the most visible means of assert-

ing one's importance was through extravagance.
The French nobility watched the rise of the bourgeoisie with a mixture of astonishment, jealousy, and apprehension. Yet there was little it could do but contain
its rage and frustration as it witnessed the erosion of
its privileges and the restructuring of the old social
order. Aristocratic courts drew closer to the flourish-
ing urban centers as an uneasy coalition of the two
classes began to form. But the spirit of the nobility
was not about to concede without resistance. There
remained a strong if slightly shaken conviction of a
privileged destiny, an elite status conferred as a
birthright, and consequently unpurchasable and untrans-
ferable. Because of its ardent desire to recodify this
status, to create a new hierarchy impervious to the
changing social climate, the nobility developed an insa-
tiable appetite for pageantry, processions, tournaments, heraldry, ritualistic ceremonies, and exclusive
societies. Beneath the pomp and splendor of all these
elaborate displays can be sensed an urgent quest for
identity, a desperate attempt to locate a secure moor-
ing in a sea of confusing and illusive values.

Evolution of Lyric Poetry in the Fourteenth Century

The radical social changes associated with the
events of the Hundred Years' War generated a resurgence
of didactic literature in France. Jean de Meung's
Roman de la Rose enjoyed wide popularity during this
period and inspired a revival of moralistic works.
Lyric poetry, however, remained on the whole stubbornly
resistant to didactic incursions. The world of the
courtly lyric from its troubadour origins tended to be
isolated from external influence. The drama of the
poem was completely self-contained, and seldom conveyed
any information concerning the poet's background,
milieu, or moral convictions. Occasionally a professional poet (for example, Colin Muset or Rutebeuf in
the thirteenth century) would allow a good-natured
comment on his poverty to slip into one of his poems,
but these exceptions were rare indeed.
By the fourteenth century, poetry and music were
becoming increasingly disassociated from each other.
The last great French lyricist to combine poetic and
musical talent was Guillaume de Machaut (ca. 1300-

1377). This poet spent most of his career as chaplain and secretary to various kings before finally retiring to Reims as canon of its famous cathedral. As the leading composer of the <u>Ars Nova</u>, the polyphonic musical style of the fourteenth century, his fame spread during his lifetime throughout France and much of Europe. Although Machaut did compose several didactic pieces called <u>dits</u> (long narrative poems), his greatest literary contribution was to establish firmly the fixed genres that were to dominate lyric poetry for a hundred years after his death. These forms included the <u>lai</u>, <u>virelai</u>, <u>chanson royale</u>, <u>complainte</u>, <u>ballade</u>, and <u>rondeau</u>, but it was the last two genres that were to gain particular favor with Charles d'Orléans and his contemporaries.

Machaut was succeeded by a number of disciples, the earliest of whom was Jean Froissart (ca. 1337-ca. 1404). Although he is better known today for the prose of his chronicles, Froissart was one of the most highly esteemed poets of his period. Like Machaut and all of the major poets of the fourteenth century, he maintained close ties with the royal courts during most of his life. A well-traveled man, he collected English as well as French patrons and included among the latter Louis d'Orléans, Charles's father (6). Froissart's poetry lacks Machaut's grace and mellifluence, for the chronicler was a rhetorician rather than a musician. Aside from serving as another link in the passage of the courtly tradition from the troubadours to the later medieval poets, Froissart's most significant poetic contribution was his cultivation of the rondeau. In all, he composed 107 examples of this form (compared with twenty-one written by Machaut), thus helping to prepare the genre for the popularity it would encounter in the fifteenth century.

Christine de Pisan (1364-ca. 1430), a later successor of Machaut, is virtually the only French poetess of the later Middle Ages to be read today. Widowed at the age of twenty-five after ten years of marriage, Christine took up writing as a means of supporting herself and her three children. Much more than either Machaut or Froissart, who both had substantial incomes from their clerical positions, Christine depended upon the generosity of her courtly public for her livelihood. In her impressive list of patrons we find again the name of Louis d'Orléans. In addition to various

lyrical compositions, her literary production includes
a biography of Charles V (who had employed her father
Thomas as his official astrologer) and numerous didactic works. In a sense she deserves to be called one of
the earliest feminists. In the quarrel of the Roman
de la Rose, the debate on the status of women inspired
by Jean de Meung's derogatory remarks, it was Christine
de Pisan who became the champion of the women's cause.
Although she was undoubtedly influenced by Machaut,
Christine acknowledged herself a disciple of Eustache
Deschamps, the man who may ultimately have exercised
the greatest influence on the course of lyric poetry in
the following century.

Deschamps (1346-1406) received his poetic formation
in Reims under the personal tutelage of Guillaume de
Machaut. Prepared by his study of law at the University of Orléans, he went on to hold a variety of administrative and diplomatic positions under Charles V and
Charles VI, including a term as royal magistrate of
Senlis. He was at one point attached as a squire to
the court of Louis d'Orléans.

Without question, Deschamps was the most prolific
poet of his century. Although his time and energy were
constantly drained by administrative duties, he managed
to compose over fifteen hundred pieces totaling close
to eighty-two thousand lines of verse. His range of
subjects extends far beyond the limited assortment of
conventional topoi. Any matter of current interest,
whether the death of a prominent figure, the birth of a
prince, or a turn in the war, he considered worth pre-
serving in ballad form. But it is particularly in his
invective against the moral corruption of society that
Deschamps excels. He chastises the rich, the greedy,
the English, the Flemish, and the pillaging bands of
French soldiers among others. Gossip, injustice, hypocrisy, and war are his most frequent targets of virulent
attack.

Deschamps's ballads often focus on the poet himself:
his relationship with society, injustices he has suffered, the declining state of his health. In this
respect he develops a pattern begun in the previous
century by Colin Muset and Rutebeuf, a concept which
one critic calls the "conscience du Moi," the "consciousness of the self" (7). In other words, while
most poets were presenting themselves in non-individual-
ized terms, their "I" standing for an entire category

of people, or even representing the whole of humanity,
a few poets were portraying themselves in a more person-
alized manner, relating specific circumstances of their
condition that set them apart from others.

Didactic, comic, often heavily satiric, Deschamps's
lyric output cannot be called the most lofty and inspired verse of the fourteenth century. His talent, in
comparison with that of his predecessors and contemporaries, has sometimes been termed mediocre.
Deschamps's most important contribution, however, lies
not in the realm of poetic talent, but in his willingness to open the lyric to subjects traditionally considered off-limits. In doing so, he not only stretched
the topical boundaries of the genre, but forced poetic
language to reshape itself in order to meet the challenge of this expansion. Thus he endowed a previously
rigid form of expression with a certain degree of elas-
ticity. To some of his contemporaries Deschamps's
poems, bearing the mark of his legal training and his
earthy attitudes, may have appeared a degradation, if
not a violation, of a long-respected poetic tradition.
Viewing his verse from a more detached perspective, we
can appreciate the extent to which he enriched and
broadened the genre, priming it for future growth.

The development of lyric verse under Deschamps and
the fifteenth-century poets who were to follow him
marked a new stage in the evolution of French poetry.
The world of the lyric, originally hermetic and uncon-
taminated by contacts with the mundane, was moving
perceptibly closer to the daily concerns of the society
for which it was written. No longer limited in scope
to the standard topoi of fin'amors, the genre was
now applied with increasing frequency to non-courtly
subjects. Attention to the material side of life and
the frailties of human nature gave rise to new strains
of skepticism and pessimism. The uplifting lyricism of
the canzo d'amors, although still present in the era
of Charles d'Orléans, found itself seriously threatened by the swelling wave of didacticism which swept
through French literature in the wake of the tumultuous
historical events of the fourteenth century.

The basic shift of orientation that we find in
fifteenth-century lyric verse is evident not only in
the significant expansion of subject matter, but in the
restructuring of poetic language. Vocabulary borrowed
from the legal and commercial professions begins to ap-

pear in a courtly context. Examples of imagery based
on political, commercial, or financial analogy may be
found in the most personal poems. The intrusion of
non-courtly language into lyric poetry attests to the
growing influence exerted by the bourgeois class. It
also attests to the genre's diminishing capacity to
retain its "purity" in the face of harsh social
realities which were becoming increasingly difficult to
escape.

Yet the desire to escape was present. And the mode
most frequently used to express this desire was lyric
verse. The courtly ideal with its emphasis on
sacrifice, honor, and transcendence of suffering was
still very close to the hearts of the nobility.
Struggling to maintain its sense of dignity amid the
chaotic events of the Hundred Years' War, the
aristocracy clung stubbornly to any remnant of
established order. In the courtly traditions of lyric
poetry this class found a distant echo of a bygone era
of chivalry. And since the nobility was still the
leading sponsor of the arts, the courtly tradition was
kept alive alongside the new poetic currents. The
survival of this "pure" strain of poetry can be
explained by the same phenomenon responsible for the
proliferation of tournaments, processions, and
ritualistic ceremonies toward the end of the Middle
Ages. The nobility was simply seeking to reennoble
itself after the debasements it had been forced to
endure. Everything reminiscent of past glory became an
object of veneration. Yet beneath this yearning for a
lost legacy of virtue and order lay a resigned
awareness that a new age was coming into its own. It
was into this world of confused values that Charles
d'Orléans was born in 1394.

Chapter Two
Biographical Sketch
The Early Years (1394–1415)

Little information exists on Charles d'Orléans's childhood. From his birth Charles spent considerably more
time in the company of his mother, Valentina, daughter
of the Duke of Milan, than in that of his father,
Louis, brother of King Charles VI. Valentina is consistently portrayed by the chroniclers of her time as a
gentle, unpretentious woman who brought to her husband's court a charming note of grace and refinement.
Louis, on the other hand, receives mixed reviews from
his contemporaries. All agree that he was not a model
of morality. Especially fond of gambling and women, he
managed to squander a large part of the family fortune
and father at least one illegitimate child. A rather
powerful political figure, Louis succeeded in acquiring
a number of enemies, the most dangerous of whom was his
ruthless cousin, Jean-sans-Peur, Duke of Burgundy.

Charles's earliest studies encompassed the seven
liberal arts which formed the core of the traditional
medieval education. Under the tutelage of Nicolas
Garbet, a master of arts and a bachelor of theology, he
and his younger brothers, Philippe and Jean, were led
through a curriculum of grammar, logic, rhetoric, arith-
metic, geometry, music, and astronomy. In addition to
his formal education, Charles was also allowed access
to his father's large library, which included works by
Aristotle, Ovid, Cicero, and Virgil, as well as the
writings of Saint Augustine and Saint Bernard. In his
mother's library he found less ponderous works which
were more apt to stimulate his imagination: Arthurian
legends, romances such as Perceval le gallois, and an
illustrated copy of Guillaume de Lorris's Roman de la
Rose.

One can hardly imagine an environment more conducive
to the development of the young poet's aesthetic sensibilities. Fairly well sheltered from the vicissitudes
of war and civil unrest, the Loire valley provided a
haven from the storm that was sweeping over much of
France. Here, surrounded by beauty and tranquillity,

Charles experienced a period of innocence and security
whose memory would help sustain him through the dark
years ahead. Here also he wrote his first poems.
There is good reason to believe that Charles was writing poetry as early as the age of ten (1). The boy's
penchant for poetry was hardly deprived of encouragement, for both his parents were patrons of the art, and
well-respected poets, including Eustache Deschamps,
were frequently received as honored visitors (2).

A chain of events beginning with Charles's marriage
to his cousin Isabelle, daughter of Charles VI and
recent widow of Richard II of England, was eventually
to threaten the well-being of the House of Orléans.
The marriage of the two youths (Charles was eleven,
Isabelle sixteen at the time) was arranged by Louis as
a tactic to strengthen his political position against
his adversaries. Jean-sans-Peur, aware of Louis's
strategy, became alarmed by this and other indications
of his shrewd cousin's increasing influence over the
mentally unstable Charles VI. The jealousy and paranoia of Jean-sans-Peur grew so intense that on November
23, 1407, the day before Charles's thirteenth birthday,
the Duke of Burgundy had Louis d'Orléans murdered in
Paris by a band of hired assassins.

Following Jean-sans-Peur's brazen admission of re-
sponsibility for his cousin's murder came a mockery of
justice in which he was officially exonerated of his
crime. Valentina, exhausted with grief and the cares
of administering the family estate while pursuing justice for her deceased husband, died on December 4,
1408, almost exactly a year after Louis's death.
Charles experienced his third loss within two years
when Isabelle died on September 13, 1409, after giving
birth to a daughter. With this series of personal
tragedies, Charles was abruptly thrust into a world of
intrigue, risk, and betrayal, a life for which no boy
of fourteen could have been prepared.

The responsibilities shouldered by the young Duke of
Orléans were enormous. Fortunately he had access to
the counsel of his father's loyal advisors and friends.
Under their guidance Charles's first decisive step came
in 1410 with his marriage to Bonne, the eleven-year-old
daughter of Bernard d'Armagnac, one of the strongest
allies of Orléans. In 1411, having strengthened his
alliance with Armagnac, Charles found himself riding
among the leaders of a sizeable military expedition

headed for Paris. The objective of the march was to display a convincing show of strength in the hope of persuading Charles VI to reconsider his hasty acquittal of Jean-sans-Peur. The campaign, however, turned out to be a dismal failure, incurring heavy losses at the hands of Parisian and Burgundian troops. Charles and his allies were eventually forced to retreat in humiliation to their own territories.

Charles was soon to experience a worse defeat, one that would become perhaps the single most decisive influence of his life. After a prolonged period of relative peace between England and France, Henry V had resolved to pursue actively his claim to the French crown. Late in the summer of 1415, he entered France with a relatively small contingent of loyal and well-tested troops. The long-awaited confrontation between the two armies came on October 25 near the village of Azincourt. The French, far outnumbering their opponents and confident of an easy victory, proved no match for the tactically superior English army with its highly skilled archers and well-trained infantry. In loss of life and morale the cost of Azincourt was a heavy one, and one which the French would continue to pay for years to come. It has been estimated that seven to ten thousand French were killed in the battle; Charles was fortunate enough to be among the fifteen hundred taken prisoner.

As one of the most valuable pieces on the chessboard (to borrow an analogy from Charles's favorite game), head of one of the most important noble families, and nephew of the king himself, the Duke of Orléans represented a prize catch for the English. Charles must have realized from the outset that his captors would not part with him easily. What he could not foresee, humiliated and despondent though he may have been, was that he would spend the next twenty-five years, over a third of his total lifetime, on foreign soil. This period of exile, for all the hardships it inflicted, afforded the elements that were to nurture a fledgling poetic talent to maturity: long periods of unbroken concentration, guaranteed isolation, and endless opportunities to exercise the imagination.

England (1415-1440)

"Imprisonment" is too harsh a word to describe

Charles's extended sojourn in England. While it is
true that he was constantly kept under close surveillance, he was treated with all the deference due to a
member of the royal family. Considered an honored
guest rather than a prisoner of war, Charles was provided a modest but comfortable existence at the Crown's
expense. In addition to the privilege of retaining a
personal servant, the duke was allowed visits from various officers of his administration, who often brought
welcome messages and mementos from home. In the early
years of his captivity much of Charles's energy was
directed toward raising the enormous sum required to
meet his ransom. His secretaries were instructed to
draw up extensive inventories evaluating the family's
financial resources. When it became apparent, however,
that he was more valuable to his captors as a bargain-
ing asset than as a potential source of revenue,
Charles gradually abandoned the struggle for his
release.

When he was not tending to routine administrative
affairs, the rest of his day was mainly divided between
game playing, reading, and composing poetry. The
library he assembled in England, close to a hundred
books according to the inventory, consisted mainly of
religious works: lives of the saints, breviaries, mis-
sals, psalters, books of hours. In addition to soli-
tary diversions, he also had numerous opportunities to
share the company of his appointed guardians and their
families. The men to whose keeping Charles was entrusted at various points during his stay in England were
all members of the nobility. They could therefore
speak, or at least understand, the native language of
their charge, a fact which must have somewhat eased his
feeling of isolation.

After spending two years in or near London, Charles
was to pass the remaining twenty-three years of his captivity in at least seven seignorial manors scattered
throughout the country, but concentrated mainly in central and south-central England. One can only speculate
on the monarchy's motives for having him transferred at
regular intervals. It has been suggested that the peri-
odic changes of residence were intended to thwart any
collusion that might develop between the hostage and
his guardians as a result of long acquaintance.

A friendship did in fact develop between the duke
and one of his appointed custodians, William de la

Pole, Earl of Suffolk, to whose care Charles was entrusted between 1432 and 1436. A former hostage himself, an admirer of French culture, and a man of refined taste who shared Charles's fondness for poetry,
Suffolk immediately took a liking to his charge. There
is no evidence that the friendship between the two men
ever threatened the earl's loyalty to England, in spite
of later accusations by his enemies (3).

It was sometime before 1436, while residing at
Suffolk's estate of Wingfield, that Charles learned of
the death of his wife Bonne (4). The grief of this
loss, compounded by nearly twenty years of accumulated
sorrows and frustrations, dealt a heavy blow to the
duke's morale. The transfer of guardianship in 1436
did little to alleviate his despair. But the tide of
the war had turned by now, and Charles's liberation was
becoming a more definite possibility. France and
England, both economically drained by the cost of sustaining large standing armies, were feeling increasing
pressure to bring the long chain of hostilities to an
end. As Charles perceived a growing hope for peace in
the air, he discovered a new source of energy and inspiration. Through a series of letters to the governments
of both countries, he repeatedly stated his willingness
to serve as a negotiator in the peace talks which he
was convinced would soon take place.

The decision to free Charles d'Orléans was not
motivated so much by compassion for his plight as by
simple political expediency. Staged as a gesture of
concession, the duke's release was intended to impress
the French with their enemy's good faith and earnest
desire to settle old grievances. The English were also
hopeful that their hostage, once released, would exert
all his influence to persuade his countrymen to put an
end to the war. On November 3, 1440, Henry VI officially declared Charles d'Orléans a free man. Charles's
first recorded words upon landing in France prove that
the long ordeal had not completely deprived him of his
sense of humor. He is said to have greeted the Duchess
of Burgundy, a woman whose intervention had been instrumental in securing his release, with the words, "Madam,
in view of what you have done to secure my deliverance,
I surrender myself as your prisoner" (5).

Among the few possessions that Charles brought back
to France was a small book embossed with his coat of
arms. This treasured volume contained those poems he

had composed in England that he considered worthy of
preservation. Although the original manuscript has
been lost, its text has been reconstructed from a
series of contemporary copies (6). We know that the
volume contained a long allegorical poem, La Retenue
d'Amours [The retinue of love] probably written before
1415; another allegorical narrative, Songe en complainte [Dream in the form of complainte] composed
in 1437; as well as eighty-three songs, four carols
(one of which is written in Latin), and ninety-six ballads including three authored by friends of the poet.
The genre in which Charles obviously felt most comfortable was the ballad, and these pieces written in exile
are undoubtedly among the most moving of all his poems.

The ballads composed in England align themselves
around two main thematic axes: love and solitude. No
definitive identification has ever been made of the woman addressed in the ballads. Charles, who refers to
her most frequently as "ma Dame," leaves few clues concerning her identity. The most credible hypothesis,
first advanced by Charles's foremost biographer, Pierre
Champion, links the dame to the poet's second wife,
Bonne d'Armagnac. A series of poems lamenting the
death of the lady (a "noble Princesse") appears to coincide with Bonne's death prior to 1436. It has also
been suggested that a number of the later ballads were
addressed to the English lady who is the subject of
Charles's songs. While the identity of the dame continues to vex and intrigue his biographers, it is of
little relevance to those who study his poetry. In concealing the lady's name, Charles is simply observing
one of the most respected laws of the courtly code.
The identity of the lady is ultimately less important
than the wealth of feelings she elicits from the poet
and the manner in which these feelings find expression.

If the link between biographical fact and literary
representation is unclear in the theme of love, the connection is immediately apparent in the case of solitude. An acute awareness of temporal and spatial separation pervades this period of Charles's poetry. Cut
off from his familiar world, plunged without prepara-
tion into an alien culture, he turned inward for consolation. The proliferation of allegorical figures in
these poems attests to the vitality of his poetic imagination, one of the few means by which he could transcend the loneliness of his isolated condition. More

than stock personifications, these figures represent
the poet's attempt to translate and record a wide range
of inner conflicts of varying intensity.

Although Charles's confinement, as previously mentioned, cannot accurately be termed imprisonment, it is
true that as a hostage in enemy hands, his freedom became severely restricted. The necessity of keeping him
under surveillance and the generally intemperate climate forced him to spend a good portion of his time in-
doors, particularly within the confines of his own
room. The chambre becomes, in fact, one of the most
frequent metaphorical representations of the poet's curtailed freedom. Unable to travel freely, Charles was
restricted to inner exploration, using poetry as a
means of probing the complexities of the human mind.

At some point, probably after Bonne's death, Charles
appears to have shown a great deal of interest in a
young lady from an aristocratic English family, possibly an acquaintance of one of his guardians. The songs
he composed in England, short poems intended to be eventually accompanied by musical notation, were composed
in her honor, and most were probably sent to her as
gifts. Precise information about this relationship is
lacking; practically all knowledge of it has been ob-
tained from internal evidence. There seems to be a connection between this lady and the one who appears in
the English poetry that some ascribe to Charles d'Orléans. This remains one of many unanswered questions concerning the period of the duke's life spent in England.

It is certain that the experience of spending over a
third of his life separated from his family, friends,
and homeland profoundly influenced the character of
Charles d'Orléans. To what extent the experience affected the course of his poetic career is a question
open to conjecture. It may be that even under normal
circumstances, his full literary potential would have
been eventually realized. It is also very possible
that without the rigors of exile, without the discipline taught by forced solitude, Charles's early inclin-
ation toward poetry would never have matured beyond the
mediocre talent demonstrated by so many of his contemporaries.

The Later Years (1440-1464)

Returning to France in 1440, Charles was immediately

caught up in a flurry of political activity. Philippe
of Burgundy, anxious to enlist his cousin's political
support, persuaded Charles to marry Marie de Clèves,
Philippe's niece. Marie was only fourteen at the time
and, according to one chronicler, a strikingly beautiful girl. Charles VII, disturbed by this hasty alliance between the Dukes of Burgundy and Orléans,
refused to welcome Charles personally when the latter
arrived in Paris a few weeks after his release. Thus
Charles was now expected to reconcile his cousins,
Charles and Philippe, as well as perform an instrumental role in initiating peace between France and England. In the first task he achieved reasonable success; the second challenge, however, far exceeded his
capabilities as a diplomat.

Having achieved all he could in the political realm,
Charles returned to Blois and settled down to his administrative duties. There remained, however, one matter
that would require extensive travel and expenditures
before it could be resolved. Through his mother he had
inherited the city and county of Asti in Lombardy, and
the Italian territory had become one of his most highly
prized holdings. While in England, Charles agreed to
place Asti in the temporary custody of Valentina's
brother, the Duke of Milan. When his uncle died in
1447, provisions of the will stipulated that Asti,
along with other territorial possessions, be left to
the Duke of Aragon, in spite of Charles's legitimate
claim to the inheritance.

In October, 1447, Charles d'Orléans, accompanied by
a modest military force, arrived in Asti where a warm
greeting awaited him. For the moment his legal claim
was vindicated. But the campaign ultimately proved of
inadequate strength to secure lasting possession of the
city, and he returned to France the following year to
seek assistance. In 1450, resigned to his loss, he completely abandoned the project.

Disenchanted by the failure of the Asti campaign,
and now relatively purged of ambition, Charles was
finally ready to retire to Blois where he would spend
the greater part of his last fifteen years. With a
well-staffed manor (eighty-seven servants at one point,
which was not an extravagant domestic staff for a man
of his rank), he was assured of a comfortable existence. The retaining household, made up largely of
well-educated young squires from good families, also

served as a ready source from which Charles could re-
cruit chess partners and participants for his poetry
competitions.

In his later years, as advancing age and poor health
gradually limited his mobility, one of Charles's greatest delights was to encourage those around him to try
their hand at verse. He would frequently offer a popular adage and solicit others to compose a ballad or rondeau using the proverb as a common point of departure.
In his personal album Charles collected many of the
poems resulting from these contests along with his own
compositions. Among the names of contributors we find
listed numerous retainers and administrative officials,
along with Charles's wife, Marie, his personal physician, Jehan Caillau, the Dukes of Burgundy, Alençon,
and other members of the nobility.

Included in Charles's personal manuscript are two
pieces by a young and (at the time) relatively unknown
poet named François Villon. The first is a ballad composed for one of the competitions at Blois, and which,
like all the other entries in this particular contest,
opens with the now famous line, "Je meurs de suef
aupres de la fontaine" ("I die of thirst beside the
fountain"). It is generally believed that Villon composed the piece in 1457 or 1458 while probably living
as a pensioned poet in Blois. (Charles is known to have
granted modest pensions to a number of "poets-in-resi-
dence.") The other poem, a lengthy eulogy of Charles's
infant daughter Marie, was written in honor of the
child's birth in 1458. Villon was twenty-seven at the
time; Charles, sixty-four.

Although the competition in which Villon participated stipulated the use of the ballad, it was the form
of the rondeau that dominated Charles's interest on his
return to France. This terse and highly musical form
served as the ideal vehicle for the cynicism and wry
humor that became increasingly pervasive in his later
poetry. These pieces cover a wide range of topics
including nature, society, love, and hypocrisy, and are
written with a subtly playful touch. The rondeau's
lilting rhythm and its melodious refrain further emphasize the levity of its subject matter. Through this
poetic medium Charles banters his friends and house
guests, ridicules young lovers, and complains good-
naturedly of the ailments of old age. The detachment
consistently maintained by the poet, as well as his un-

rivaled mastery of the form, lend these little poems a
distinctive charm.

   In 1462, having recently fathered two daughters, the
duke finally saw the arrival of his long-awaited male
heir. His son would eventually become king of France
and rule under the name of Louis XII. But he would
have few if any memories of his father. Charles's
health was rapidly declining. In late December of
1464, while returning from business in Tours, he was unexpectedly forced to stop in the castle of Amboise.
The exact nature of his illness is not recorded, but
the generally poor state of his health and the rigors
of winter travel were undoubtedly contributing factors.
During the early morning of January 5, 1465, Charles
d'Orléans died at the age of seventy. In one of his
rondeaux are found two verses that the poet could well
have chosen for his epitaph:

>   Je ne suis pas de sez gens
>   A qui Fortune plaist et rit. (7)
>
>   (I am not one of those people
>   Upon whom Fortune smiles.)

But Fortune, for all the hardships she had inflicted
upon her victim, had at least granted him the gift of a
long life.

Chapter Three
The Early Ballad Cycle
History and Form of the Ballad

The word ballade (not to be confused with the narrative ballads found in the English, Spanish, and other
European literary traditions) entered French via Provençal from the late Latin ballare, meaning "to dance"
(1). Like most medieval lyric forms, the ballad had
its beginnings in popular song, and evidence of its
musical origin is readily apparent in the genre's use
of the refrain. Prior to the fourteenth century, the
term ballade was applied to a wide variety of poetic
forms. Largely as a result of Guillaume de Machaut's
influence, the ballad had become a clearly defined
genre by the middle of the fourteenth century (2).

Along with the other formes fixes, especially the
virelay and rondeau, the ballad enjoyed wide popularity
throughout the fourteenth and fifteenth centuries.
Already imported to England where such poets as
Chaucer, Gower, and Lydgate succumbed to its growing
appeal, the ballad found favor with Froissart and
Deschamps, and later with their successors: Christine
de Pisan, Alain Chartier, Henri Baude, and others. The
undisputed masters of the form, and those who most
fully explored its potentialities, were Charles
d'Orléans and François Villon. Although rejected by
the poets of the Pléiade, the ballad form was used by
Marot, La Fontaine, Voiture, and by several members of
the Parnassian movement.

The structural model on which most ballads are based
consists of three stanzas plus a short envoi, the part
in which the poem is dispatched (envoyé) to the
patron or loved one for whom it is destined (3). All
stanzas are constructed on an identical rhyme scheme
and end with a one-verse refrain. The envoi repeats
the versification of the second half of the stanza and
contains the refrain as the closing verse of the poem.
The number of syllables per line generally corresponds
to the number of lines per stanza, although considerable latitude is permitted in the observation of this
rule. The most common stanzaic form is the huitain

(eight verses, the basic unit of Villon's Testament, and the form most frequently used by Charles d'Orléans), followed by the dizain (ten verses). Among the most common variations of the standard ballad form, one finds the six-stanza double ballad and the five-stanza chant royal.

Until Charles's release from England, the ballad clearly held a predominant position in his poetic corpus. Drawn by the challenges of this highly structured form, the poet experimented freely with its possibilities for variation. He produced, among other interesting mutations, a five-syllable verse and an eleven-verse stanza. Rather than constricting the expression of his ideas within the rigid boundaries that the ballad would seem to impose, he molds the form around the ideas, refusing to sacrifice depth of thought or sharpness of imagery to the demands of his chosen medium.

Images of Confinement

In the prison of love, a topos found throughout the development of the courtly lyric, the figurative incarceration of the poet represents the helpless state of the martyred lover, a helplessness which, moreover, the victim readily accepts. Guillaume de Machaut, the most influential lyric poet of the fourteenth century, uses the motif in typical courtly fashion:

> S'Amours me tient en sa prison joieuse,
> Je me rens pris sans faire nul contraire. (4)
>
> (If love holds me in his joyful prison,
> I surrender myself without resistance.)

The prison joieuse symbolizes the tyranny of love over its subjects, a tyranny which the poet, like Tristan, willingly embraces.

Structures of containment, including the prison, surface recurrently in Charles's ballads, generally appearing in the traditional courtly context, but sometimes charged with a more personal significance. For these references to restricted freedom often evoke, either directly or indirectly, the poet's condition as a hostage of war. Explicit allusions to his actual confinement are rare. One such factual statement is found in the envoi of a ballad protesting the injustices of Fortune:

> De balader j'ay beau loisir,
> Autres deduis me sont cassez;
> Prisonnier suis, d'Amour martir.
> Helas! et n'est-ce pas assez?
> (1:61)

> (For writing ballads I have ample time,
> Other amusements are forbidden me;
> A prisoner am I, a martyr of love.
> Alas! and is this not enough?)

The starkness of the pronouncement "Prisonnier suis" is somewhat tempered by the balancing half of the verse. Like the prisoner, the martyr of Love is another popular courtly mask. Juxtaposed then with <u>martir</u>, <u>prisonnier</u> takes on a shade of metaphorical coloring which softens the impact of the initial declaration.

In the envoi of another ballad Charles abandons the courtly posture for a stoic pose, allowing a degree of detachment to intervene:

> Fruit suis d'yver qui a meins de tendresse
> Que fruit d'esté; si suis en garnison,
> Pour amolir ma trop verde duresse,
> Mis pour meurir ou feurre de prison!
> (1:131)

> (I am a winter fruit that is less tender
> Than summer fruit; and I am in storage
> To soften my very green hardness,
> Set to ripen in the straw of prison!)

Knowing the duke's physical existence not to have been lacking in basic comforts, we should refrain from the temptation to give too literal a reading to the "straw of prison." The intended image is rather that of a bin or storage area lined with straw, a place where immature fruit could be left to ripen. According to an earlier statement in the same poem, the <u>fruit d'yver</u> has been placed in storage by providential design. The resignation and the note of hope (for even the hardest fruit will eventually ripen and be removed) stand in marked contrast to the tone of despair heard in the previously cited ballad.

A more graphic reference to the poet's environment occurs in one of the numerous poems celebrating Saint Valentine's Day:

> Le beau souleil, le jour saint Valentin
> Qui apportoit sa chandelle alumee,
> N'a pas long temps, entra un bien matin
> Priveement en ma chambre fermee.
>
> (1:91)

> (The beautiful sun, on Saint Valentine's Day,
> Carrying his lighted candle,
> One fine morning, not long ago,
> Familiarly entered my closed room.)

Taken with the visual image of the second verse, the chambre fermee suggests a darkened (perhaps shuttered) room whose obscurity is penetrated by a soft ray of sunlight. On the other hand, the phrase may also be translated as "locked room." Although this allusion to confinement, again, need not be taken at face value, it inevitably elicits the image of the prison.

More often than the poet himself, it is his heart that finds itself within restricted boundaries:

> Pour ce que veoir ne vous puis,
> Mon cueur se complaint jours et nuis,
> Belle, nompareille de France,
> Et m'a chargié de vous escrire
> Qu'il n'a pas tout ce qu'il desire
> En la prison de Desplaisance.
>
> (1:46)

> (Because I cannot see you,
> My heart complains day and night,
> Lovely lady, peerless one of France,
> And has charged me to write you
> That he does not have all he desires
> In the prison of Discontent.)

After its initial appearance in the first verse (where the first person pronoun is understood to be the subject of puis) the "I" of the poem steps aside, yielding the stage to the principal actor, the heart. As the latter appropriates the role of the poet, the "I" is reduced to a secondary status, acting as a kind of secretary in carrying out the orders of a superior. By fragmenting his personality into two distinct entities, one acting as an intermediary for the other, the poet partially dissociates himself from the emotional conflict represented by the prison de Desplaisance. If not restricted by prison walls, the heart is often depicted within the boundaries of another confining structure such as a room or fortress:

> Je ne crains Dangier ne les siens,
> Car j'ay garny la forteresse
> Ou mon cueur a retrait ses biens,
> De Reconfort et de Lyesse;
>
> (1:48)

> (I do not fear Dominion or his men,
> For I have fortified my fortress,
> Where my heart has withdrawn his
>   possessions,
> With Consolation and Joy;)

This extended metaphor of the fortified stronghold exemplifies the military imagery so prevalent in Charles's early ballads. The heart, by retreating to the safety of the fortress, is in effect voluntarily committing itself to confinement while bracing for the expected assault. The biens carried into the stronghold represent the poet's ultimate treasure, his store of memories; this accounts for the soothing presence of Reconfort and Lyesse.

The choice of the confining structure, corresponding to the mood of the poem, is significant in itself:

> Mon cueur est devenu hermite
> En l'ermitage de Pensee;
>
> (1:64)

> (My heart has become a hermit
> In the hermitage of Thought;)

The "hermitage of Thought" strikes a somber, almost tragic note which will be echoed throughout the poem. On the basis of the few passages cited above, we can see a definite pattern emerging. In each case the heart is forced into confinement by external forces which it

is powerless to control. Although each passage implies
isolation, the nuance varies according to the choice of
imagery. The prison connotes a punitive purpose as
well as a sense of justice (providential design). The
fortress suggests a protective element to the seclusion, a retreat of the heart and its memories into a
refuge of solace. Implied in the ermitage de Pensee,
with its evident spiritual dimension, is an attitude of
meditation which seeks to transcend rather than escape
adverse circumstances. More than mere variations on a
theme, these images represent three distinct responses
to the state of exile: resignation, escape, and transcendence.

Given that Charles d'Orléans spent a substantial
portion of his life as a hostage of war, it may seem
surprising to find in his poems so few direct allusions
to this important fact. Villon, in contrast, makes no
secret of his brief stay in the prison of Thibault
d'Aussigny. Granted, Villon's period of incarceration
was much harsher than Charles's exile in terms of physical conditions. It must also be remembered that these
poets wrote in two different registers. Villon's
style, characterized by a dazzling richness of vocabulary and multiplicity of tones, allows great flexibility and adapts itself well to the incursion of autobiographical data. Charles d'Orléans, on the other hand,
chose (at least during the first half of his poetic
career) to compose within the framework of the courtly
mode, a mode not well suited to the conveyance of autobiographical information. This is not to say that
Charles's ballads are no more than highly polished specimens of courtly lyric devoid of any personal touch.
Were this true, his poetry would never have attracted
much more attention than that of his contemporaries,
many of whom were accomplished craftsmen in the art of
verse. In the case of the metaphor of the confined
heart, the various images discussed above are clearly
charged with a personal relevance not found in conventional handling of the topos. These images not only
carry the expected association of helplessness, but
also convincingly convey an acute sense of solitude.

Exploring Inner Space: The Magic Mirror

The exile ballads of Charles d'Orléans are characterized by a deceptively simple surface concealing the-

matic and semantic patterns of remarkable complexity.
The immediate impression is one of well-turned phrases,
polished delivery, and adept manipulation of poetic
effects. But also discernible, even at first reading,
is a rich harmony, the skillful orchestration of a variety of stylistic and thematic components. No amount of
textual analysis can "reconstruct" this harmony, any
more than the dissection of a musical score into its
individual notes will convey a notion of melody. But
by focusing on a single ballad in its entirety, we may
gain some appreciation of the delicate nature of the
poet's craft.

Poem 35 of Champion's edition opens with a stanza
whose syntax is disarmingly direct, almost proselike:

> J'ay ou tresor de ma pensee
> Un miroeur qu'ay acheté.
> Amour, en l'annee passee,
> Le me vendy, de sa bonté.
> Ou quel voy tousjours la beauté
> De celle que l'en doit nommer,
> Par droit, la plus belle de France.
> Grant bien me fait a m'y mirer,
> En attendant Bonne Esperance.
>   (1:54)

> (I have in the treasury of my thought
> A mirror which I bought.
> Love, last year,
> Sold it to me, out of kindness.
> In it I always see the beauty
> Of the one who must be called,
> By all rights, the fairest of France.
> It does me great good to look at myself
>   there,
> While waiting for Good Hope.)

The mirror whose existence is revealed in the second
verse is, on several levels, an empty image. First, at
least at the moment of its initial appearance, it does
not contain any visible reflection. Second, although
the mirror is obviously intended to function in a figurative sense, its immediate context yields no clues
which would allow us to interpret its meaning. The following two verses appear at first to shed some light on
the mystery of the mirror. But the fact that the ob-

ject was purchased from Love (portrayed here as a kind
of benevolent peddler) contributes little to help us
decipher the enigma. The temporal specification, "en
l'annee passee," seemingly delimits an actual and perhaps consequential occurrence in the poet's life. Yet
the circumstances surrounding the event remain inaccessible to the reader. Having been allowed entry into
that most secret and intimate space, the "treasury of
thought," we meet immediately with a locked door. Our
transgression of the poet's privacy therefore is only
superficial.
     At this point an image suddenly appears in the mir-
ror. But rather than share the image by attempting to
re-create it, the poet is content to leave the voyeur-
reader watching him gaze into the mirror. In the final
two verses of the stanza we realize that he is now star-
ing at his own reflection. The doubling effect of the
mirror is skillfully underscored by the phonetic repetition of m'y mirer. Rich in semantic possibilities,
the verb mirer may designate either the simple act of
peering into a mirror, or may indicate a degree of
admiration or contemplation on the part of the viewer.
As the image of the woman is replaced by that of the
poet, a sort of narcissistic substitution occurs.
Again the versatility of the verb comes into play,
mirer meaning "to reflect" as well as "to look at."
From a different origin the word signifies "to heal"
(related to mire, doctor), and this reading is borne
out by the context of the word, and further developed
in the following stanza. Finally, whether by chance or
design, mirer and its etymological cousin, mirouer,
appear in the penultimate and second verse respectively, creating a mirror-like symmetry.
     It is possible to read the eighth verse in such a
way as to minimize its narcissistic connotations. The
image of the woman, although appearing before that of
the poet in the sequential progression of the stanza,
does not necessarily take chronological precedence over
the latter. Thus there exists the possibility that the
two images are viewed simultaneously, one superimposed
on the other. One of the mirror's magical qualities
then would be the power to reunite poet and mistress in
likeness if not in person. This interpretation would
account for the salutary effect (grant bien) produced
by looking into the mirror. Bonne Esperance, incidentally, could be taken as a transparent allusion to

Charles's wife, Bonne.

The second stanza parallels the first by beginning with the physical object, underscoring its personal value for the poet, then proceeding to extol its extraordinary attributes:

> Je n'ay chose qui tant m'agree,
> Ne dont tiegne si grant chierté,
> Car, en ma dure destinee,
> Maintesfoiz m'a reconforté;
> Ne mon cueur n'a jamais santé,
> Fors quant il y peut regarder
> Des yeulx de Joyeuse Plaisance;
> Il s'y esbat pour temps passer,
> En attendant Bonne Esperance.
>   (1:55)

> (I have no other thing which pleases me so,
> Nor which I hold so dear,
> For in the course of my hard fate,
> Many a time has it comforted me;
> Nor is my heart ever in good health
> Except when he can look into it
> Through the eyes of Joyful Pleasure;
> He amuses himself there to pass away time,
> While waiting for Good Hope.)

The image of the woman has now completely disappeared and will not resurface in the remainder of the ballad. By the end of the stanza it is clear that a definite shift of focus has occurred. While the first stanza concentrates on the object of the mirror and what the poet sees reflected in it, the second centers on the actual act of looking. Continuing to gaze into the mirror, the poet steps outside the act to observe the tableau from a distance. The reader, slightly disoriented by now, finds himself watching the poet watch himself gazing at his own reflection.

The poem's meaning hinges ultimately on our assessment of the poet's magic glass. One intriguing interpretation is suggested by Stendhal's famous epigraph: "Un roman: c'est un miroir qu'on promène le long du chemin." ("A novel: it is a mirror moved alongside the road.") If Charles's mirror (stationary, in contrast to that of Stendhal) is taken to represent his art, the ballad at once becomes more accessible. The

poet's fascination with his treasure, its therapeutic
effects, its ability to produce images of his loved
one, all could be interpreted as attributes of the
poetic act. Moreover, the mirror's capacity to repro-
duce images, allowing the viewer to see himself as if
he were seeing another person, reinforces the partici-
pant/observer dichotomy that characterizes the persona
of Charles's exile poetry.

In the closing stanza the focus returns to the mirror itself:

> Advis m'est, chascune journee
> Que m'y mire, qu'en verité
> Toute doleur si m'est ostee;
> Pour ce, de bonne voulenté,
> Par le conseil de Leauté,
> Mettre le vueil et enfermer
> Ou coffre de ma souvenance,
> Pour plus seurement le garder,
> En attendant Bonne Esperance.
>   (1:55)

> (It seems to me, each day
> That I look at myself there, that in truth
> All sorrow is lifted from me;
> Because of this, in good faith,
> On the advice of Loyalty,
> I want to put it away and shut it
> In the coffer of my memory,
> To keep it more safely,
> While waiting for Good Hope.)

Having removed it from the "treasury" of his thought to
display and admire it, the poet now locks the mirror
securely away in the "coffer" of his memory, bringing
the ballad full cycle. Form reflecting content, the
closing of the poem coincides neatly with the closing
of the coffer.

Perhaps the most puzzling element of the poem is not
the mirror, but the female image which appears for only
an instant, to be immediately replaced by the poet's
own image (assuming they do not appear simultaneously).
Sudden as the transition may be, it occurs nonetheless
in a smooth and natural manner; for the mirror, having
momentarily assumed supernatural powers, is merely
returning to its intended function, i.e., reflecting

the image of the viewer. Contemplation of the Other ultimately becomes contemplation of the Self. Whatever symbolic value one wishes to attach to the mirror--poetry, memory, imagination--the inescapable effect of the object is to produce self-knowledge. It is precisely for this quality, and for the peace and joy associated with such knowledge, that the mirror is so highly valued by the poet. Without forcing the text, one may read the ballad as a meditation upon the act of contemplation. This introverted orientation, the "looking at the looking," emerges as one of the dominant perspectives of the early ballad cycle.

At the deepest level, this is a poem about illusion; for the mirror is basically an instrument of deception, designed to create a convincing mirage, a verisimilar reproduction of what actually exists. The importance of illusion in these ballads cannot be overstated. Memory reunites the poet with those he loves, filling the void of the moment with their presence. Allegorical figures share his company and help restore order to the chaotic wanderings of his thoughts. Hope, his strongest and most loyal ally, constantly holds before his eyes the chance for freedom. The world of these poems is peopled with phantoms and visions. Yet there is no air of morbidity here, for these illusions represent the distillation of all that is vital and positive within the creative force.

The "I" and the Heart

By now it should be evident that the "I" of the exile ballads does not necessarily represent the whole poetic personality, i.e., the self-image projected by the poet. This personality is more often fragmented into various components--"I," the heart, Memory, Hope-- all of which somehow fuse into a cohesive entity. As the poetic personality dissociates into its constituent parts, there exists the continual risk that these elements will suddenly emancipate themselves from the poet's grasp. The challenge of the "game," and it is a game at which Charles is an expert player, is to complicate the network of personality fragments without losing control over their proliferation.

If the poetic "I" cannot automatically be identified with the integrated personality of Charles d'Orléans, then which facet of the poet does it in fact represent?

The most revealing way in which the "I" defines itself
is in its relationship with the heart. The dichotomy
is not always based on opposition:

> Je sens ces motz mon cueur percer
> Si doulcement, que je ne sauroye
> Le confort, au vray, vous mander
> Que vostre message m'envoye.
>
> (1:56)

> (I feel these words pierce my heart
> So sweetly that I could not,
> In truth, express to you the comfort
> That your message sends me.)

No effort is made here to dissociate the heart from the
first person of the poem. Instead, the former emerges
as an exension of the latter, a localization of emotional sensitivity, and as such retains its traditional signification as a courtly topos. The lady's message
makes its impact directly on the poet's heart without
the interference of any third party. Stripped of allegorical status, cueur merely serves its expected function as a refinement of je.
  This conventional depiction of the heart does not,
however, represent Charles's favorite handling of the
motif. Personification offers greater breadth for his
introspective wanderings:

> L'autr'ier alay mon cueur veoir,
> Pour savoir comment se portoit;
> Si trouvay avec lui Espoir
> Qui doulcement le confortoit
>
> (1:56)

> (The other day I went to see my heart,
> To learn how he was feeling;
> And with him I found Hope
> Who was gently comforting him)

Espoir has come to console the grieving heart (the
latter fittingly clad in black) and eventually succeeds
in reviving his sagging spirit. The spatial distance
separating poet and heart is paralleled by a degree of
detachment exhibited in the first two verses. The casual tone of these opening lines indicates a kind of

neighborly concern bordering on indifference. Throughout the rest of the ballad the poet remains true to the purpose of his visit ("mon cueur veoir"), observing the scene between cueur and Espoir, but carefully refraining from intrusion. Discreetly effaced, the first person of the poem positions itself as an inconspicuous observer of the little drama being enacted. Like the spectator of a play, he is able to legitimately invade the privacy of an intimate moment without violating its sanctity. From his privileged vantage point the poet records the scene, translating emotional turmoil into allegorical imagery. At the end of the poem he addresses his belle maistresse, reminding her of her power to uplift his heart. From passive observer, the first person becomes an intercessor, an advocate pleading his client's case.

Watching its various trials, the poet is sometimes moved to address his heart directly:

> Bien sçay, mon cueur, que faulx Dangier
> Vous fait mainte paine souffrir;
> Car il vous fait trop eslongnier
> Celle qui est vostre desir.
>
> (1:71)

> (Well I know, my heart, that false Dominion
> Makes you suffer many a pain,
> For he keeps you far from
> The one who is your desire.)

In the passage quoted at the beginning of this section, a sensory connection was established between the "I" and the heart ("Je sens ces motz mon cueur percer"), revealing one as an integral part of the other. Now the heart's pain is recognized by a different mode of perception: "Bien sçay..." With the substitution of intellect for feeling a gap opens, and this distance is underscored by the use of the formal vous, the form of address consistently used by the poet in addressing his heart. As the heart is endowed with a separate identity, the boundaries of its suffering become more clearly delineated. Standing outside these boundaries, the poetic "I" is, momentarily at least, immune to pain.

At one point the "I" explicitly defines its relationship with the heart:

Je lui dis: "Mon cueur, je vous pry,
Ne vueilliez croire ne penser
Que moy, qui vous suy vray amy,
Vous veuille mensonges trouver,
Pour en vain vous reconforter."
                                            (1:80)

(I said to him, "My heart, I beg you,
Neither think nor believe
That I, who am your true friend,
Wish to invent lies
To comfort you in vain.")

The bond between je and cueur, according to the
speaker of this poem, is one of friendship, a camaraderie
ie tempered with a certain respectful distance, as indicated by the use of vous. Yet within this relationship exists the possibility of deceit. This explains
je's protest of loyalty and honesty in anticipation
of the heart's mistrust. The news brought to the
heart, the fact that the poet's lady has recovered from
a serious illness, and the heart's reaction to this
announcement provide the focus of the ballad. Again
the "I" is relegated to a secondary role. Serving the
function of secretary or messenger, he merely relays
the message to its intended recipient.
  Despite the self-effacing behavior typically exhibited by the poetic "I" in its relation with the heart,
moments of assertion are not altogether lacking. In the
following passage, having rebuked Loyal Espoir and
Joyeuse Pensee for "sleeping too long," the poet
urges them to turn their attention to his heart:

Vous ferez bien d'un peu le resjoïr,
Tristesse s'est avecques lui logiee;
Ne lui vueillez a son besoing faillir.
                                            (1:41)

(You will do well to cheer him a bit,
Sadness has come to lodge with him;
Do not fail him in his hour of need.)

After repeated pleas, the "I" addresses the lady at the
end of the poem, again interceding on behalf of the

heart. It is interesting to note that throughout the ballads no direct communication is ever established between lady and heart. All messages (like Charles's actual correspondence with France) are relayed through an intermediary.

Reduced to simplest terms, the dichotomy of je and cueur represents reason versus feeling. The je designates that part of the poet that stands back from emotional turmoil and calmly surveys the situation. It approaches inner discord analytically, incisively isolates the core of the conflict, and verbalizes the problem using symbolic language (5). The heart, on the other hand, sensitive, vulnerable, and incapable of detaching itself from the immediacy of emotional upheaval, epitomizes the "younger" side of the personality. Adolescently moody, impulsive, and self-centered, the heart lacks the wisdom of its "older" counterpart.

With his penchant for personification, Charles could have easily chosen a purely allegorical mode for depicting the opposition of reason and emotion. The incorporation of reason into the "I" is not an arbitrary decision. By separating the intellect from the feelings that tend to contaminate it, the poet achieves a kind of spiritual purification. The refined consciousness that results from this distillation becomes, momentarily at least, the core of the poet's being, as demonstrated by the use of the first person pronoun. Charles Baudelaire in a famous sonnet creates a similar effect of transcendence: "Sois sage, O ma Douleur, et tiens-toi plus tranquille." ("Be calm, O my Sorrow, and keep more still.") Once freed of its emotional burden, the persona can address itself with absolute serenity to the problem of suffering.

Although the "I" frequently addresses the heart with words of encouragement, admonishment, advice, and gentle reproach, the latter rarely answers. The act of speech, as an attempt to translate feelings into language and thus impose a semblance of order, lies beyond the realm of the heart. Its reticence, its refusal or inability to respond to the intellect, may itself be construed as a response of helplessness or defiance. The harangue of reason ultimately proves ineffectual, and the "I," except for occasional attempts at intercession, remains consigned to the powerless role of observer.

The Ballad as Letter;
Reflections on the Act of Writing

Throughout his exile in England, Charles maintained
contact with his homeland by means of a steady exchange
of written messages. His secretaries, traveling under
the protection of safeconducts, moved freely from one
country to another, carrying official messages as well
as those of a more personal nature. This reliable method of communication served two important functions.
First, it allowed the duke to follow political develop-
ments in France, kept him apprised of economic conditions in his own province, and enabled him to govern
his domain by proxy. Equally important, it provided a
vital link between the hostage and his friends and family, a means of conveying mutual reassurance and pledges
of continued loyalty and affection.

That Charles enjoyed corresponding in verse with his
acquaintances is evident from numerous copies of letter-ballads brought back from England in his personal
manuscript. Several replies written in versified form
have been recorded as well, enabling us to follow some
exchanges in their proper chronological sequence. In a
ballad composed in 1432 Charles congratulates a fellow
hostage, the Duke of Bourbon, upon his release and asks
that he relay a message to Bonne. In another, he humor-
ously informs an unnamed acquaintance that in spite of
rumors to the contrary, he is not in fact yet dead.
Exchanging a series of ballads with the Duke of Burgundy in 1439 and 1440, he requests help in securing
his release, then thanks his cousin for his assistance.

Also included in Charles's manuscript was a large
number of ballads addressed to an anonymous lady,
presumably his wife, Bonne (6). Approached as specimens of epistolary correspondence, the poems yield dis-
appointingly little in the way of autobiographical
data. Still, it is clear that they were written to
serve a communicative as well as a literary function.
They confirm the state of the poet's health and mind,
convey a minimum of circumstantial information, acknowledge receipt of correspondence, and frequently encourage the lady to continue writing. Charles's desire to
keep the text within the elevated realm of courtly
poetry prevents his verse from degenerating into a pro-

saic account of mundane affairs, the kind of subject
matter which fills so many of the mediocre ballads of
his predecessor, Eustache Deschamps. It is also largely due to his discreet suppression of extraneous information that our knowledge of Charles's exile contains
so many lacunae.

In response to his lady's request that he write her
a ballad Charles protests the inadequacy of writing as
a means of expressing the intensity of his feelings:

> Se vouloye raconter plainnement
> En cest escript mon ennieux martire,
> Trop long seroit; pour ce certainnement
> J'aymasse mieulx de bouche le vous dire.
> (1:37)

> (If I wished to fully recount
> In this writing my grievous suffering,
> It would be too long; because of this
> I certainly would prefer to tell you in
>   person.)

More commonly applied to legal documents than literary
works, the term escript draws attention to the physical nature of the text, the paper and ink of which it
is composed. A second legal term, de bouche, differ-
entiating oral from written deposition, reinforces the
status of the text as a kind of official testimony.
The trop long of the third verse may be read at least
two different ways. Either the full disclosure of
Charles's suffering would be too painful for the lady,
or too taxing to be faced by the poet. A third possibility is that the adjectival phrase applies to the
fact of the suffering rather than to its narration,
hence stating the impossibility of compressing the experience into literary form.

The letter-ballads frequently end with a request
that the correspondence be sustained. It is especially
in these pleas for communication, the classic symptom
of homesickness, that one senses the depth of the
poet's loneliness:

> Jeune, gente, nompareille Princesse,
> Puis que ne puis veoir vostre jeunesse,
> De m'escrire ne vous vueillez lasser;
> (1:59)

(Young, lovely, peerless Princess,
Since I am not able to see your youth,
Do not tire of writing to me;)

Appearing in two consecutive verses, _jeune_ and
jeunesse underscore the lady's age. (Bonne, five
years Charles's junior, was only sixteen at the time of
her husband's capture.) Despite the fact that the poet
makes no reference to the passage of time, a temporal
element manages nonetheless to creep in, coloring the
poem with a subtle shade of melancholy. Again Charles
allows a certain latitude of interpretation, based this
time on the ambiguous use of _jeunesse_. The word may
be taken as an allusion to the physical attributes of
the lady (her freshness, the bloom of her complexion),
and as such would be roughly equivalent to "youthful
beauty." Or it may refer to a period of her life that
the exiled poet is prevented from sharing. This second
reading gives the verse a somber, if not tragic, quality. In either case, the word carries temporal connotations, and the poet's separation from the lady's
jeunesse clearly implies a loss. The letters requested from the lady will in some small measure compensate
for this deprivation.

Although none of these letters, the other half of
the correspondence, has survived, we are occasionally
given a tantalizing glimpse of their contents. The
refrain of one ballad is comprised of a phrase alleged-
ly quoted from a recently received missive:

Pour m'oster de merencolie,
M'escrivy amoureusement:
"C'estes vous de qui suis amye."
                              (1:69)

(To free me from melancholy,
She wrote to me lovingly:
"It is you whose lover I am.")

There is no way of knowing whether the refrain renders
the text verbatim or whether the statement has been mod-
ified to be made less prosaic. In any case, the brevity of the phrase as well as its context in this letter-
ballad suggest that even if the poet has tampered with
the citation, he has not departed significantly from
its original content. Another purported quotation,

substantially longer, may be read as a versified paraphrase:

> Car escript m'avez pour m'oster
> Ennuy qui trop me guerroye:
> "Mon seul amy, mon bien, ma joye,
> Cellui que sur tous amer veulx,
> Je vous pry que soyez joyeux
> En esperant que brief vous voye."
> (1:56)

> (For you have written to rid me of
> Sorrow who wages war on me with great
>   vigor:
> "My only love, my wealth, my joy,
> He whom I love above all others,
> I beseech you to be joyful
> While waiting until I see you soon.")

Again, the degree to which the text of the letter has
been altered cannot be determined, but we have no reason to doubt that these verses were inspired by, if not
patterned after, an authentic excerpt of correspondence.

The written word is rendered sacred not only by the
reverence of the poet for his art, but by the yearning
of the man for his loved one, a yearning whose expression must, by force of circumstances, be restricted to
written form. Given its privileged status, it is only
natural that the act of writing, like all that the poet
most deeply cherishes, be transferred into the sanctum
of the heart:

> J'ay en mon cueur joyeusement
> Escript, afin que ne l'oublie,
> Ce refrain qu'ayme chierement:
> C'est vous de qui suis amye.
> (1:70)

> (In my heart I have joyfully
> Written, so that I will not forget it,
> This refrain which I love so dearly:
> It is you whose lover I am.)

Already elevated by its metamorphosis from prose communication to poetic refrain, the message of love now be-

comes further consecrated as an inscription engraved
upon the poet's heart. In another case Charles again
internalizes the act of writing, associating it this
time with the process of thought:

> J'ay mis en escript mes souhais
> Ou plus parfont de mon penser;
> (1:71)

> (I have put my desires into writing
> In the deepest part of my thoughts;)

The first verse has a distinctively testamentary ring,
and the first four words are in fact repeated in
another ballad in conjunction with the writing of an
imaginary testament (7). Inscriptions, testaments,
poetry, all confer upon the written word a special
power, one for which this poet shows the deepest
respect.

Finding Charles's love ballads anthologized among a
variety of poems composed by the same author under different circumstances and at different periods of his
life, one is apt to forget that these intimate pieces
were not in fact originally intended for "public con-
sumption." Here Charles's poetry sets itself apart
from the mainstream of courtly tradition (8). The love
songs of the troubadours and trouvères, although addressed on the surface to the poet's lady, were actually designed with an eye to performance. The counterfeit intimacy required by courtly canon merely provided
a pretext for the poet to display his virtuosity. Written for one particular woman, and charged with conveying intense feelings of longing and loneliness,
Charles's love ballads portray a genuine struggle
against despair. Only many years after their composition were the poems finally released from the poet's
notebook (9).

Perhaps the most important axiom of modern criticism
is that any given text should be approached from within; the external circumstances relating to its composition are generally regarded as superfluous if not completely irrelevant. Without contradicting the basic
validity of this principle, an occasional case may
still be made for the importance of historical context.
Our appreciation of these poems can only be enhanced
by an awareness of their dual nature as examples of

literary and epistolary discourse.

Dover

One of the most significant and readily apparent results of the Hundred Years' War was the rise of a nationalistic sentiment among the French. Courageous military leaders such as Du Guesclin and Jeanne d'Arc had fired the popular imagination while providing a focal point for the new groundswell of patriotic enthusiasm. Whatever damage the war may have inflicted on the French land and spirit, it at least left the country with a stronger cohesiveness and unity of purpose. Patriotism, although not a dominant theme in Charles's poetry, does occasionally surface in his work, revealing another facet of his character.

In May, 1433, Charles had good reason to be optimistic about his chances for freedom. It was during this month that he was sent to Dover to help negotiate a permanent truce. Charles himself, along with his friend the Earl of Suffolk, had been instrumental in arranging the meeting and had promised to use all his influence in urging his countrymen to attend. Now, reunited with his cousin, the Duke of Bourbon, whom he had not seen since they were both captured at Azincourt, he was eagerly awaiting the arrival of the French ambassadors. The meeting would never take place. After six anxious weeks without a sign of the delegation, Charles would return to Ampthill. The Dauphin, obviously uninterested by the proposed treaty, had not even deigned to respond.

The period of waiting in Dover, although ending in bitter disappointment for the French hostages, did inspire what has become one of the best-known French poems of the fifteenth century:

> En regardant vers le païs de France,
> Un jour m'avint, a Dovre sur la mer,
> Qu'il me souvint de la doulce plaisance
> Que souloye oudit pays trouver;
> Si commençay de cueur a souspirer,
> Combien certes que grant bien me faisoit
> De voir France que mon cueur amer doit.
> (1:122)

(Looking toward the land of France,

> It happened one day, at Dover on the sea,
> That I remembered the sweet pleasure
> Which I used to find in that land.
> And I began to sigh from my heart,
> Although it certainly did me much good
> To see France that my heart must love.)

Standing high above the Atlantic on the chalk cliffs of
Dover, Charles received his first glimpse of the country he had not seen for eighteen years. But seen by
the unaided eye from a distance of some twenty miles
across the channel, France appears, even on the clear-
est of days, as no more than a pale strip on the hori-
zon. It is interesting, therefore, that the poet initially pictures himself as looking toward rather than
directly at his native land. The opening verse empha-
sizes not the scene actually visualized but (as in the
poem about the mirror) the act of looking itself. This
is further underlined by the placement of the verb at
the beginning of the verse, a practice he rarely uses
in opening other ballads. The contemplative stance of
the poet as he positions himself at the very outermost
edge of his island-prison may be taken as a symbolic
posture. More important than what he actually sees is
the wish, the yearning to see, a desire strong enough
to bridge the gap with imagination where sight fails.

In facing his native land, the poet is also in a
very immediate sense confronting his past. The bridging of spatial distance thus naturally leads to the
bridging of temporal distance with the introduction of
memory in the third verse. The gazing outward, paradoxically but predictably, has become a gazing within.
Given the emotional intensity underlying the poem and
the upheaval one would expect from such a direct confrontation of past and present, the most remarkable
feature of this piece is its restraint. This self-
control cannot have been imposed without considerable
effort. For beneath the calm surface of the verse,
feeling and form are vying for control, the former
threatening to destabilize the latter. Yet if form
ultimately dominates, it does so without altogether
stifling the "sighs of the heart." Here is yet another
demonstration of the poet's exceptional sense of
balance.

The second stanza centers on the hope for peace

which then leads to thoughts of return in the last stanza:

> Alors chargay en la nef d'Esperance
> Tous mes souhaitz, en leur priant d'aler
> Oultre la mer, sans faire demourance,
> Et a France de me recommander.
> Or nous doint Dieu bonne paix sans tarder!
> Adonc auray loisir, mais qu'ainsi soit,
> De voir France que mon cueur amer doit.

> (Then I loaded in the ship of Hope
> All my wishes, bidding them go
> Beyond the sea, without delay,
> And to remember me to France.
> Now may God without tarrying grant us
>   sweet peace!
> Then will I have leisure, but may it be so,
> To see France that my heart must love.)

As the poem develops, the distance separating the poet from his native shore gradually and inconspicuously diminishes. In the first stanza he progresses from "looking toward" to "seeing" France. Having established visual contact, he then communicates with his country by means of the nef d'Esperance. The souhaitz, whose mission is to remember the poet to France, refer possibly to poems or messages dispatched during Charles's stay in Dover. In transmitting wishes, whether in material or purely mental form, the poet is sending ahead a part of himself as an emissary. The successive stages of contact culminate with Charles's projected return to France. In the refrain of the third stanza the verb voir takes on a new nuance. While in the first two stanzas it indicated a perspective grounded on the English side of the channel, it now designates a vantage point on French soil from which the poet may leisurely view his country.

The poem ends with a reflection on peace and war:

> Paix est tresor qu'on ne puet trop loer.
> Je hé guerre, point ne la doy prisier;
> Destourbé m'a long temps, soit tort ou
>   droit,
> De voir France que mon cueur amer doit!

> (Peace is a treasure one cannot praise
>   too much.
> I hate war, I ought not esteem it in
>   the least;
> It has long prevented me, be it right
>   or wrong,
> From seeing France that my heart must
>   love!)

The words pays and paix, the two key nouns in the
poem, are linked by more than phonetic association, for
the former will not be seen by the poet until the latter is achieved. "Je hé guerre," a flatly unpoetic
declaration, stands out from the rest of the ballad as
a bald statement of contempt. The staccato effect of
this phrase, especially perceptible after the melodious
smoothness of the preceding verse, breaks the rhythmic
flow of the poem, accentuating the disruptive force of
war. After fleeting incursions into the past and
future, the poem ends squarely in the present with its
one overbearing reality, the fact of war and exile.

Contained within this famous poem is a clearly discernible seed of nationalistic identity. The poet's
wishes are instructed to remember him to a personified
France, and it is difficult to miss the note of pride
in the refrain. The verb doit, whether or not intended to function in a strictly prescriptive sense, de-
notes an obvious moral obligation. But rather than
interpret the poem, as some French editors have chauvin-
istically done, as a heartfelt cry of patriotism, one
may more justifiably read it as the lyrically charged
yet controlled expression of the yearning of a
dépaysé for his family, friends, and homeland.

A Personal Loss

Toward the end of his detainment in England, the
tranquillity of Charles's well-ordered existence was
shattered by the news of a death. The victim, to whom
he refers only as "la noble Princesse," is generally
believed to have been his wife, Bonne, who died of
unspecified causes prior to 1436. The illness preceding her death, the news of the tragic event, and its
immediate repercussions form the nucleus of a series of
nine poems (10). These ballads, charged with unmistakable intensity, detach themselves thematically from the

main body of Charles's early poetry. Taken together,
they chronicle a journey through the various stages of
grief: shock, a sense of loss, despair, resignation.

Informed that his lady has fallen ill, the poet reacts with immediate apprehension:

> Helas! Helas! qui a laissié entrer
> Devers mon cueur Doloreuse Nouvelle?
> Conté lui a plainement, sans celer,
> Que sa Dame, la tresplaisant et belle,
> Qu'il a long temps tresloyaument servie,
> Est a present en griefve maladie;
>
> (1:79)

> (Alas! Alas! who has allowed
> Painful News to enter my heart's presence.
> She has told him frankly, hiding nothing,
> That his Lady, pleasing and lovely,
> Whom he has long and loyally served,
> Is at present gravely ill;)

Alarmed by the manner in which <u>cueur</u> reacts to the
message, the poet visits his heart in an unsuccessful
effort to relieve his fears. Again the conflict of reason and emotion is represented in the <u>je</u>/<u>cueur</u>
dichotomy. By the end of the poem the threat of death
has been transferred from the lady to the poet's heart,
physically stricken by the news.

The next ballad in the series celebrates the lady's
apparent recovery. The poet immediately brings his
heart the good tidings, and the latter, in a rare moment of joy, is moved to speech:

> "Il est temps que rappelle
> Espoir, qui delaissié m'avoit;
> Saint Gabriel, bonne nouvelle!"
>
> (1:81)

> ("It is time I call back
> Hope who had abandoned me;
> Saint Gabriel, good news!")

Filled with elation and a feeling of relief, the ballad
attests the gravity of the lady's illness and the apprehension with which the poet had been awaiting the final
outcome. Lured into a false sense of security, Charles

was totally unprepared for the next message he would receive. Whether through a relapse or an unexpected complication, the illness proved more virulent than suspected.

With the tragic news obviously still fresh in mind, the poet's first response comes more as a protest than a lament:

> Las! Mort qui t'a fait si hardie,
> De prendre la noble Princesse
> Qui estoit mon confort, ma vie,
> Mon bien, mon plaisir, ma richesse!
>   (1:81)

> (Alas! Death, how could you be so bold
> As to take the noble Princess
> Who was my comfort, my life,
> My good, my pleasure, my wealth!)

Restrained within the bounds of poetic discourse lies a cry mingling anger, shock, and disbelief. The intensity of the poet's rage and grief, voiced in uncharacteristically stark and forceful language, rises immediately to the surface. Forgotten are the play between the poet and his heart, wanderings through the elaborate architecture of the mind, metaphorical representations of internal conflict, and the companionship of Hope, Memory, and Thought. In this ominous moment the poet stands alone confronting death. Appearing here for the first time in Charles's poetry, Mort is, unlike the other allegorical figures that people the ballads, a total stranger. The use of the familiar form of address suggests not intimacy as much as the scorn of a man issuing a challenge to an opponent. This challenge materializes in the second half of the stanza when the poet, half defiantly, half pleadingly, urges Death to take him as well.

Although this poem with its scarcity of imagery and lack of technical refinement may not be one of Charles's most polished pieces, it does effectively convey his deep sense of loss:

> Las! je suy seul, sans compaignie!
> Adieu ma Dame, ma lyesse!
>   (1:82)

(Alas! I am alone, without company!
Farewell, my Lady, my joy!)

In time he will be able to express the loss in more
sophisticated terms. For the moment his emotions can
only take the very simplest and most direct form of
expression. The fact that he would even attempt under
such adverse conditions to translate his feelings into
verse speaks strongly for Charles's need to write.
More than a mere avocation, poetry permitted him a
means of establishing landmarks by which he could later
retrace the various stages of his spiritual journey.
Whether through dedication to his poetic journal or
simply out of long-imposed discipline, he felt compelled to record this particularly difficult experience, even at its most painful moment.

The next poem in the series is inspired by a memory
associated with the celebration of the new year:

> Je me souloye pourpenser
> Au commencement de l'annee
> Quel don je pourroye donner
> A ma dame la bien amee.
> (1:83)

> (I used to reflect,
> At the beginning of the year,
> On what gift I might give
> My dearly beloved Lady.)

Wishing to <u>garder la costume</u> ("keep the tradition"),
he has decided that his gift this year will be a requiem mass. But the poem itself contains a more personal
gift, a brief and moving prayer for the salvation of
the lady's soul, ending with the poem's refrain: "Je
pry Dieu qu'il en ait l'ame" ("I pray God that he keep
her soul"). Although the woman is never directly addressed, one is left with the distinct impression that
the ballad was written for her as a kind of final farewell. The tone of solemnity, well suited to the ritualistic quality of the poem, never becomes so heavy as to
be oppressive. Composure and equilibrium again control
the creative process.

In a moment of meditation, the still painful memory
prompts a consideration of the fragility of human life,

a favorite preoccupation of fifteenth-century thought.
Drawing on Celtic and classical mythology for his com-
parisons, the poet elevates his lady to near legendary
status:

> Ou vieil temps grant renom couroit
> De Creseide, Yseud, Elaine
> Et maintes autres qu'on nommoit
> Parfaittes en beauté haultaine.
>   (1:85)

> (In the old days great fame spread
> Of Cressida, Iseut, Helen,
> And many others who were named
> Perfect in highest beauty.)

The poem goes on to lament the cruelty of Death who re-
spects not even the most perfect specimens of human
beauty. This particular selection of female personages
should not be considered completely random. Each woman
can be said to have, in some sense, abandoned her husband or lover, whether through infidelity, submission
to moral obligation, or abduction. Like Helen,
Charles's mistress has been abducted, never to be returned. (The Ubi sunt theme also inspired a ballad
by Deschamps and the famous "Ballade des dames du temps
jadis" by Villon; its various treatments by these poets
provide an interesting comparison.)

Days of celebration tend to evoke the memory of the
deceased: New Year's Day, Saint Valentine's Day, the
first of May. In commemoration of May Day Charles once
participated in a courtly diversion which stirred old
memories and provided the occasion for another ballad.
Each member of the company was apparently instructed to
choose between the sign of the leaf and the flower,
with the understanding that an emblem of the selection
would be worn throughout the year. Charles, without
great deliberation, opts for the leaf. He then proceeds, in characteristic fashion, to interpret his
choice as a symbolic gesture. Having lost his most precious flower to Death, he states that his heart desires
no other. The poem ends with a reflection on the transience of all mortal beings:

> Il n'est fueille ne fleur qui dure
> Que pour un temps, car esprouvee

> J'ay la chose que j'ay contee,
> Comme lors fut mon aventure.
>
> (1:87)

> (There is neither leaf nor flower that endures
> Longer than but for a time,
> For I have experienced the thing I have told,
> As it has been my fortune.)

In a sequel to this ballad the flower appears before
the poet in a dream, reproaching him for his infidelity. He defends himself vigorously, claiming that his
choice cannot be fairly taken as a sign of fading loyalty. Some have seen in this poem evidence of a new love
in Charles's life. Without entirely ruling out this
possibility, we must bear in mind that such an assumption is based, at best, on a speculative reading of an
ambiguous text.

Saint Valentine's Day (the birds' first day of mating, according to an ancient belief) offers Charles
another bitter reminder of his loss. Waking to the
sound of birdsong, and realizing that he is hearing a
chorus of mating calls, the poet experiences an acute
sense of loneliness:

> Chascun de vous a per qui lui agree,
> Et point n'en ay, car Mort, qui m'a trahy,
> A prins mon per......
>
> (1:92)

> (Each of you has a pleasing mate,
> And I have none, for Death, who betrayed me,
> Has taken my mate......)

Isolated from the natural order, represented here by
the mating songs of the birds, the poet finds himself
condemned to an unnatural state of solitude. The poem
succeeds in capturing an especially poignant moment, a
sensorial association of almost Proustian intensity.
Leaving behind the illusory world of sleep, Charles
awakens, literally and figuratively, to the brutal reality he has briefly managed to elude. But harsh though
the realization may be, it is mixed inextricably with
elements of physical beauty--the soft light of dawn,
the natural music of birdsong--and the sweet and gentle
quality of the moment further deepens its extraordinary

sadness. As consciousness succeeds intuition, the
poet's melancholy finds justification in the fact that
he, a man alone, has awakened to a day of human and
animal pairing.

If the poet's lost per was in fact his wife (as
all evidence strongly suggests), it is certain that
Charles's suffering was compounded by his exclusion
from her funeral in France. Deprived of the ritual
which would have allowed him to take formal leave of
his loved one, he re-creates the event, drawing on the
resources of his imagination:

> J'ay fait l'obseque de ma Dame
> Dedans le moustier amoureux,
> Et le service pour son ame
> A chanté Penser Doloreux;
> Mains sierges de Soupirs Piteux
> Ont esté en son luminaire;
>   (1:95)

> (I have celebrated my Lady's funeral mass
> In the lovers' chapel,
> And the prayer for her soul
> Was sung by Sorrowful Thought;
> Many candles of Pitiful Sighs
> Were in her candelabrum;)

At first reading one might assume the piece to have
been written close to the time of the funeral. According to Champion, however, the ballad was written at
least a year after Bonne's death. The composed tone of
the poem, its controlled development, and highly elaborated allegorical imagery, all suggest a significant
lapse of time separating this ballad from the spontaneous cry of grief, "Las! Mort..." Feelings once too
strong to be restrained have gradually subsided, and
their expression now takes a more complex form. What
we are witnessing is not only the re-creation of the
lady's funeral, but also the reenactment of one stage
of the poet's suffering. Soupirs Piteux and Penser
Doloreux, once very immediate parts of the grieving
process, are now disguised as candles and a priest.
Like the ritual of the funeral, poetry serves here to
order a potentially disruptive experience, giving it a
sense of form and meaning. By celebrating the lady's
funeral mass in his mind, the poet demonstrates that he

has finally come to terms with her death, and has successfully integrated the event into the inner world
which is both the source and the object of his poetic
inspiration.

Chapter Four
The *Complainte* to France

At the age of thirty-nine, having spent practically half of his life in England, Charles d'Orléans composed a long poem addressed to his native country. This piece, bearing no title, is written in the form of a complainte, a term designating any long poem written on a pious or tragic theme. One of his longest works, the poem contains ten stanzas of nine verses apiece, each stanza ending on the refrain:

> Trescretien, franc royaume de France!

> (Very Christian, noble kingdom of France!)

Written in 1433, the same year in which the famous ballad was written at Dover, this is unquestionably Charles's most patriotic work. But it is not the product of a zealous patriot who can find no fault with his country. It is instead a critical appraisal of the present state of France, her misfortunes, her failings, her sins, all lamented by a man who firmly believes that his country has been reserved for a nobler destiny.

The intimate bond between the poet and his country is established in the first verse with the familiar tu form of address. (The lady of Charles's love poetry, by comparison, is consistently addressed as vous.) The poem opens with a nostalgic reference to the country's former reputation:

> France, jadis on te souloit nommer,
> En tous pays, le tresor de noblesse,
> Car un chascun povoit en toy trouver
> Bonté, honneur, loyauté, gentillesse,
> Clergie, sens, courtoisie, proesse.
> (1:258)

> (France, you were once called
> In all countries, the treasure of nobility,

> For everyone could find in you
> Goodness, honor, loyalty, nobility,
> Learning, sense, courtliness, prowess.)

The words _jadis_ and <u>en tous pays</u> create a breadth
of historical and geographical scope, lending a certain
epic dimension to the poem. The historical imperative,
the need to fulfill an illustrious destiny foreshadowed
long ago, will become one of the two major thematic
threads of the poem. Goodness, honor, and the other
six qualities listed as the cornerstones of the country's past reputation are also the virtues theoretical-
ly represented by the nobility. Charles, in fact, is
not addressing his nation in its totality, the France
of the peasantry, the France of the bourgeoisie, of the
clergy, but specifically that social class to which he
belongs and which, in political terms at least, is most
responsible for the direction the country has taken.
The stanza finishes by contrasting the past glory of
France with her present state of ruin, noting the
poet's chagrin at this loss of prestige and honor.

Having reminded France of the obligations imposed by
such a noble heritage, Charles proceeds to elucidate
the cause of her present misfortune. Her collapse, he
claims, has been brought about by a state of collective
sin:

> Ton grant ourgueil, glotonnie, peresse,
> Couvoitise, sans justice tenir,
> Et luxure, dont as eu abondance,
> Ont pourchacié vers Dieu de te punir,
> (1:258)

> (Your great pride, gluttony, sloth,
> Greed, without observing moderation,
> And lust, which you have had in abundance,
> Have caused God to punish you,)

Listed here we find five of the seven deadly sins. The
belief that the current war was an act of divine punishment brought on by rampant moral corruption was a view
widely held by French theologians, and served as the
basis for countless chastising sermons. Charles's <u>com-</u>
<u>plainte</u> is, in fact, dominated by a strikingly homilet-
ic tone. The degeneration of France is seen by the
poet as a twofold process. First, national honor has

been reduced to a hollow concept. But more important,
the French sense of dignity has been severely eroded at
a personal level. Here is the second major theme of
the poem. The betrayal of the country's heritage parallels a deeper betrayal, one which, in the eyes of the
duke and many others, is perceived to be at the heart
of the country's recent ruin.

The poet's intention, however, is not to flatly con-
demn his country's failings, but to show how they might
be corrected. Redress is possible, he points out,
through the means of divine grace:

> Ne te veuilles pour tant desesperer,
> Car Dieu est plain de merci, a largesse.
> (1:259)

> (Do not, however, despair,
> For God is full of generous mercy.)

If the war is to be interpreted as divine design, then
it follows that the punishment is not an end in itself.
Rather it is meant to awaken in the Christian citizens
of France an awareness of their sinful state of existence in order that they may repent and reform.
Charles entreats his country to seek God's mercy, but
do so with Humility as her advocate. The only means by
which France can extricate herself from her present dis-
tress, he is convinced, is through a sincere desire for
atonement. Furthermore, this expiation must be undertaken with absolute faith in Christ:

> Entierement metz en lui ta fiance,
> Pour toy et tous, voulu en crois mourir,
> (1:259)

> (Put all your trust in him,
> For you and all others he was willing to die
> on the cross,)

There is nothing bombastic or self-righteous in the
poet's advice to his country. He speaks with all the
gentleness of a concerned priest who has just taken an
especially painful confession.

The call for humility is paradoxically followed by
an appeal to nationalistic pride:

Souviengne toy comment voult ordonner
Que criasses Montjoye, par liesse,
Et qu'en escu d'azur deusses porter
Trois fleurs de lis d'or...

(1:259)

(Remember how He ordained
That you cry "Montjoye" with joy,
And that you bear on an azure shield
Three fleurs-de-lis of gold...)

This pride differs from the <u>grant ourgueil</u> so vehemently condemned in the poem's second stanza. Charles is not advocating a strengthening of personal self-esteem, but a cognizance of the privileged status of France, her divinely ordained mission. The tone of gentle remonstrance now swells into a rallying call. <u>Montjoye</u>, the ancient battle cry of the French army, and the fleur-de-lis, the royal emblem carried into battle on the banners and shields of the French troops, evoke stirring images of military engagement. But in the exuberance inspired by memories of past triumphs, the religious thread of the poem is not lost. <u>Montjoye</u> in the <u>Chanson de Roland</u> is, after all, as much a Christian as a French battle cry. And the fleur-de-lis is a symbol rich in religious associations. The emblem, according to popular belief, was originally given to Clovis by an angel in commemoration of his conversion to Christianity. Charles V fixed the number of flowers at three in honor of the Trinity. The lily flower itself was equated with purity and associated with the Virgin whom it often symbolized. The celebration of military exploits eventually takes the poet back to his premise: all events, victories and defeats, are brought about by the hand of God.

The fleur-de-lis and its connection with royalty leads to the mention of another symbol associated with the monarchy, the unction used in anointing French kings at their coronation. Like the fleur-de-lis, this oil was said to have been heaven sent, delivered, according to the legend, by a dove. The enumeration of the country's sacred gifts is completed by a reference to holy relics, an abundance of which was then to be found in France:

> Et, plus qu'a nul, t'a voulu sa richesse
> De reliques et corps sains departir;
> Tout le monde en a la congnoissance.
>
> (1:259)

> (And with you more than anyone else,
> He chose to share his wealth of relics
>   and holy bodies;
> Everyone has knowledge of this.)

The battle cry of <u>Montjoye</u>, the emblem of the fleur-
de-lis, and the holy relics are all signs of divine
sanction, material proof of the elite destiny for which
France has been chosen. These are the country's true
riches (<u>richesse</u>, v.41, <u>enrichir</u>, v.35). At a time
when his country's treasury is practically depleted,
Charles points to a far more important source of
wealth, the divine blessings bestowed upon France long
before the present war, a covenant that offers the promise of salvation to those who will hold it in reverent
esteem.

France, Charles continues, is the "right arm" of
Rome and holds a highly respected seat in the papal
court. But the honor is one she does not merit in her
present state of disgrace:

> Et pour ce dois fort pleurer et gemir,
> Quant tu desplais a Dieu qui tant t'avance
> En tous estas, lequel deusses cherir,
>
> (1:260)

> (And because of this you must weep greatly
>   and sigh,
> When you displease God who favors you so
> In all conditions, He whom you should
>   dearly love,)

It should be understood that the weeping and sighing
are not the predicted consequences of an inevitable
recognition of sinfulness. The verb <u>dois</u> functions
instead as a clear imperative, indicating there is a
choice to be made. Underlying Charles's impassioned
plea for contrition is the belief that France cannot
look to past achievements and promises of glory as a
guarantee of salvation. He recalls her illustrious
heritage only to emphasize the spiritual corruption

that has supplanted honor and virtue. The reestablish-
ment of discarded values along with sincere atonement
are, in the poet's judgment, the only means by which
redemption may be achieved.

Turning to the <u>Chanson de Roland</u> for examples of
courageous and selfless devotion to high ideals,
Charles continues to praise the past grandeur of
France:

> Quelz champions souloit en toy trouver
> Crestienté. Ja ne fault que l'expresse:
> Charlemeine, Rolant et Olivier,
> En sont tesmoings;
>
> (1:260)

> (What champions Christianity used to find in you!
> I hardly need to say it:
> Charlemagne, Roland, and Olivier
> Bear witness to this;)

To this list is added the name of Saint Louis who, like
the other legendary and historical figures, won his
fame as an ardent adversary of the Saracens. At the
moment that this poem was composed, France, incidentally, had a new Christian champion, and one who would
eventually outstrip all others in popularity. It may
seem strange that Charles should omit Jeanne d'Arc from
his list. It was she, after all, who had freed his own
city of Orléans from the hands of the English in 1429,
winning a crucial victory which would become a turning
point in the war. Her absence from the assembly of
French heroes may be explained by several factors. In
the short time that had elapsed since her execution
Jeanne's fame had not yet gained sufficient propor-
tions, in Charles's eyes at least, to allow her a place
among the majestic company of such men as Charlemagne
and Saint Louis. Her exclusion may also be explained
by her sex and humble origins. But a more important
obstacle is to be found in her contemporaneity. A
scant two years separate her death from the composition
of this poem. To admit her into the saintly ranks of
national heroes would invalidate Charles's claim that
French heroism, like French virtue and piety, no longer
exists.

In structure as well as style this <u>complainte</u> re-
sembles a sermon, echoing in condensed <u>versified</u> form

the rhetorical eloquence of the pulpit. Like a well-
constructed sermon, the poem is carefully designed to
steer its audience through a carefully ordered series
of revelations, each of which is calculated to inspire
a desired reaction. The poet has succinctly presented
his thesis in the first three stanzas of the poem.
This thesis, namely, that the future of a great country
is now threatened by the decay of its spiritual values,
is then amplified in the three succeeding stanzas.
Examples drawn from history and legend contrast the
grandeur of the past with the misery of the present.
Having completed the prefatory and expository sections
of his discourse, Charles now prepares the delivery of
the dramatic plea reserved for the end of the poem.

Alternating between a tone of supplication and admonishment, the poet directs his country on a course of
redemption. The first step is to pay proper homage to
those who have sacrificed their lives in the service of
their country:

> Tous tes meffais metz paine d'amender,
> Faisant chanter et dire mainte messe
> Pour les ames de ceulx qui ont l'aspresse
> De dure mort souffert, pour te servir;
>   (1:260)

> (Strive to amend all your misdeeds,
> By having sung and said many a mass
> For the souls of those who have
> Suffered the asperity of a hard death
>   to serve you;)

The requiem masses, it is hoped, will restore a reverence for the price at which the country's heritage was
purchased and is maintained. Placed in a proper spirit
of humility and communion, the suppliants will then be
ready to ask forgiveness for their sins:

> Dieu a les bras ouvers pour t'acoler,
> Prest d'oublier ta vie percheresse;
> Requier pardon,....
>   (1:260)

> (God has his arms open to embrace you,
> Ready to forget your sinful life;
> Seek [His] forgiveness,...)

Once France has acknowledged her sins and shown true
penitence, the Virgin and all the French saints will
intercede on her behalf. But it is essential that the
country first awaken to its plight and shake off the
evil slumber into which it has fallen:

> Ne veuilles plus en ton pechié dormir,
> (1:261)

> (Do not sleep in your sin any longer,)

Now, in the final stanza, the poet identifies himself
and makes his last and most urgent appeal. This he
formulates as a prayer. He asks that before old age is
upon him he may witness "le temps de paix" ("the time
of peace") for which he longs with all his heart, and
that he may see all his nation's sufferings quickly
cease. The prayer, although ostensibly motivated by
concern for France, is obviously invested with a strong
element of self-interest, for the advent of peace will
bring his own sufferings, as well as those of his country, to an end.

Exactly what use, if any, Charles intended to make
of the poem is not known. Perhaps it was copied and
sent to various influential parties in France. It is
just as likely that it never left the poet's notebook.
In spite of its obvious chauvinism, it would not be
entirely fair to call the complainte a propagandistic
piece. There is a sincerity, an earnestness about the
poem that cannot be ignored. Aside from its significance in Charles's poetic corpus, the work merits attention as one of the earliest French examples of patriotic poetry. Ronsard and DuBellay, each in his own way,
will take up the theme of patriotism, the latter, like
Charles d'Orléans, writing from the vantage point of a
foreign country. In addition, the poem offers an
insight of historical interest, presenting what one member of the French nobility perceived to be the broadest
implications of the war with England. Isolated from
the war for almost twenty years, and unable to exert
any influence upon its outcome, this man could view the
conflict with a degree of detachment unavailable to his
countrymen. Beyond the entanglement of political intrigue he discerned a more basic cause for his country's downfall. France, as he saw it, had simply fall-
en out of harmony with her historical tradition and

spiritual duty. What he advocates in this poem, with
its curious mixture of Christian humility and patriotic
fervor, is not military strength or artful diplomacy.
Instead, he counsels prayer and penitence. This complainte is not a harangue, but a heartfelt plea.

Chapter Five
The Narrative Poems
La Retinue d'amours

Besides hundreds of short lyric pieces, Charles d'Orléans also left two thematically related allegorical poems of substantial length. These works, too extensive to be included in anthologies of medieval French poetry, have been consigned to relative obscurity. The earlier of the two allegories, Retinue d'amours [The retinue of love] cannot be dated with certainty (1). We know only that it was composed sometime prior to Charles's capture at Azincourt in 1415. The work, obviously the product of an inexperienced poet, relates in rambling fashion a young man's first encounter with love.

Awakened one morning by Youth, the poet is told that he is about to meet the Lord of Love. Although somewhat apprehensive, he reluctantly lets himself be led to Love's manor where he is greeted by various members of the royal retinue. Charles eventually makes a bashful appearance before Love who good-naturedly teases the youth, poking fun at his innocence. At the lord's bidding, Pleasing Beauty fires an arrow at the victim while Love, much amused, urges the young man to protect himself. Youth unsuccessfully attempts to intercede on behalf of her defenseless charge. Finally Beauty, in a gesture of maternal sympathy, places the poet's head on her lap and persuades him to yield to her charm. After swearing to the ten commandments of love, the poet's allegiance to his new lord is made official in a letter of retainment drawn up by Love's secretary, Good Faith. A copy of the act, dated Saint Valentine's Day, is appended to the main body of the poem.

The youth of the poet is underscored at several points in the development of the allegory. Love addresses him as enfant, and the letter of retainment refers to him as "Charles, a present jeune d'ans" ("presently young of years"). The narrator is consistently addressed with the familiar form of the second person, as a child would normally be addressed by an adult. Throughout the poem one has the impression of viewing a grown-up world through the eyes of a child. Beneath the thin courtly disguise a genuine adolescent awkwardness and sensitivity to ridicule are readily discernible.

Even a cursory analysis of the poem's stylistic features reveals evidence of an amateur hand. Except for the letter of retainment, the poem consists of two hundred decasyllabic rhyming couplets arranged with monotonous regularity in ten-line stanzas. Numerous facile rhymes and minor mechanical flaws further attest to the poet's lack of expertise. His use of allegory bears the unmistakable stamp of Guillaume de Lorris's Roman de la Rose. Still, despite its unsophisticated versification and patent defects, the poem contains a promise of talent which must have been apparent to the older members of the young duke's entourage.

Several facts suggest that Retinue d'amours may have been inspired by Charles's relationship with his first wife, Isabelle, who died in childbirth in 1409. If the poem in fact depicts an actual experience, and is not completely fictitious, it is reasonable to assume that Plaisant Beauté represents a real woman. Charles addresses her as princesse, and she is clearly older than he is. These facts coincide with Isabelle's royal standing and her seniority of five years over the poet. The poem describes Charles's first experience with love and would therefore appear more applicable to his relationship with Isabelle than to a subsequent relationship. According to the letter of retainment, the poem was completed on Valentine's Day and was quite possibly intended as a gift to the woman portrayed by Plaisant Beauté. It should be pointed out that if the Retinue was composed before Isabelle's death, it must be accepted as the precocious work of a poet not yet fifteen years old. The lack of worldly and poetic experience demonstrated in the poem is entirely consistent with the adolescent viewpoint one would expect of so young an author.

The circumstantial evidence presented above remains, of course, far from irrefutable. It has been suggested that Plaisant Beauté represents Charles's second wife, and the possibility also exists that the Retinue is nothing less than a complete fabrication, the elaborately constructed fantasy of an active adolescent imagination. If unreliable as a source of biographical data, the work does prove revealing as a literary arti-

fact, enabling us to trace various poetic patterns to
the seminal stage of their evolution. The most prominent feature of Charles's poetry foreshadowed in the
Retinue is a heavy reliance on the allegorical mode.
Another equally important characteristic of his work,
especially conspicuous in the post-exile verse, will be
the use of humor. Although not intended as a humorous
piece, the Retinue does contain occasional light
moments. When told that he is about to be led into the
presence of Love, the poet feebly protests:

> Trop jenne suy pour porter si grant fais,
> Il vaut trop mieulx que je me tiegne en pais.
> (1:3)

> (I am too young to bear so great a burden,
> I would be much better off if I kept my peace
>   of mind.)

The combination of wisdom and humor, issuing so unexpectedly from the mouth of this serious boy, will repeatedly make itself felt in the aged poet's musings on the
folly of love.

Songe en complainte: Themes and Structure

In 1437 Charles composed his longest and most ambitious poem, a 550-verse sequel to Retinue d'amours.
Unlike its predecessor, Songe en complainte [Dream in
the form of a complainte] demonstrates a solid mastery of poetic technique. The poem merits attention
not only for its unusual length, but also for its importance as a philosophical statement made at a turning
point in the poet's life.

The first section, comprised of twenty-two eight-
verse stanzas, or huitains, opens with the poet's
preparations for sleep after an especially tiring day.
Once the obligatory stage setting has been completed,
we are plunged directly into the symbolic world of
dream in which the remainder of the poem unfolds. An
old man appears before the narrator and identifies himself as Aage. Here is the first clue to the central
preoccupation of the poem—the poet's attempt to concep-
tualize himself within the framework of human time.
The old man reviews Charles's past, laments his lack of
restraint while under the tutelage of Jennesse

("Youth"), and urges that he now preserve his honor by
abandoning Love:

> Car en descort sont Amours et Vieillesse:
> Nul ne les puet a leur gré bien servir.
> Amour vous doit pour escusé tenir,
> Puisque la Mort a prins vostre maistresse.
>
> (1:100)

> (For Love and Old Age are in discord,
> No one can serve them both well.
> Love must consider you excused,
> Since Death has taken your mistress.)

Although Aage points out that old men in love quickly
become targets of ridicule, considerable persuasion is
necessary before the poet resigns himself to renouncing
the cause of love. The old man reassures the narrator
that his decision is a wise one and will be respectful-
ly interpreted as an act of loyalty to his lost mistress. Using feudalistic terminology, Aage advises
the poet that he ask to be released from his oath of
allegiance to Love and humbly request that his heart,
given as a gage ("pledge"), be returned. The poet is
not to listen to Fortune, who will do her best to deter
him from the recommended course of action.

The dream proper ends here, but the rest of the narrative takes place in a dreamlike dimension, and the
title reminds us that the entire poem is in fact to be
considered songe. Trembling like a leaf (his own
analogy), the narrator awakens to find himself torn by
indecision. In spite of the persuasive speech of
Aage, he is reluctant to follow the latter's advice.
To do so would signify a personal defeat, the betrayal
of a vitality not yet ready to be subdued. But counter-
balancing feelings of youthful vigor is a growing sense
of weariness which ultimately wins out. Already distan-
cing himself from his past, Charles muses on the role
of love in his life:

> Je sçay par cueur ce mestier bien a plain,
> Et m'a longtemps esté si agreable
> Qu'il me sembloit qu'il n'estoit bien mondain
> Fors en Amours, ne riens si honnorable.
>
> (1:103)

> (I know full well this trade by heart,
> And it was long so pleasing to me
> That I thought there was no worldly good
> Except in Love, nor anything so honorable.)

Memories of pleasure quickly become mixed with painful recollections, and the poet announces his decision with renewed resolve. As the first section of the narrative closes, he is preparing to write a petition to be brought before <u>Amours</u> on the occasion of the next holiday.

At this point the text of the petition (v. 177-274) is introduced into the poem. The request, addressed jointly to "Dieu Cupido et Venus la deese," is couched in legalistic language and sets forth in logical sequence the various arguments supporting the poet's plea. Following this quasi-legal exposition, the narrative line resumes with a series of four ballads (275-370) grouped under the collective title, "La Departie d'Amours en ballades" [The departure from Love (related) in ballads]. Following his plan, the narrator appears before Love and formally presents his petition. His lord offers his condolences on the death of Charles's mistress, and urges that he let reason prevail over grief: "Moustrez vous homme, non pas beste" ("Show yourself a man, not an animal"). If the poet will attempt a new conquest, he may be assured of Love's support. But such an eventuality cannot be envisioned by Love's vassal, who resolutely adheres to his demand. He knows too well the price of attachment:

> Ce me seroit trop grant folie,
> Quant demourer puis en repos,
> De reprandre merencolie:
> (1:110)

> (It would be sheer madness,
> When I could remain at peace,
> To take up melancholy again:)

The supplicant humbly but firmly reminds his lord of the loyal service he has rendered and repeats the request that he be released from further obligation. Finally, recognizing his servant's steadfast purpose and the legitimacy of his claim, Love gives his con-

sent. An official quittance ("letter of exemption")
will be drawn up and presented to Love's parlement
("council") for formal ratification. After assembling
and duly consulting the advisory body, Love has the
quittance prepared and promptly delivered to his vassal. In a classic gesture of feudal submission,
Charles kneels before his lord awaiting the return of
his heart. Taking it from a jewel box, Love then
offers the object, wrapped in black silk, to its right-
ful owner:

> En mon sain le mist doulcement,
> Pour en faire ce que vouldroye.
> (1:112)

> (In my breast he gently placed it,
> To do with as I pleased.)

Following this highly ritualized scene, a second doc-
ument, the letter of exemption passed by Love's council, is introduced (374–414). The year 1437 is given
in the letter's conclusion as the date of issue. The
final narrative section, comprised of three ballads
(415–486), relates the actual separation from Love and
subsequent events, and concludes the "Departie
d'Amours." Blinded with tears at the moment of taking
leave, and therefore unable to see his way, the narrator requires the assistance of Comfort whom Love as-
signs as his guide. Confort, at the poet's request,
leads him to the manor of Nonchaloir ("Indifference")
where the poet once lived as a child. The governor of
the manor, Passe Temps, warmly welcomes his guest,
and is delighted to learn that he wishes to make Nonchaloir his permanent residence. Charles then com-
poses a letter to Love explaining his intention and
instructs Comfort to carry the message with him on his
return. The text of the letter (487–550), the third of
the series of "supporting documents," ends by situating
the poem within its historical and symbolic contexts:

> Escript ce jour troisieme, vers le soir,
> En novembre, ou lieu de Nonchaloir.
> Le bien vostre, Charles, duc d'Orlians,
> Qui jadis fut l'un de voz vrais servans.
> (1:118)

>   (Written toward the evening, on the third
>   Of November, in the place called Indifference.
>   Yours truly, Charles, Duke of Orléans,
>   Who was once one of your loyal servants.)

The final verse, tinged with nostalgia, defines the poet both in terms of his past and present relationship to Love, and encapsulates the message of the entire letter.

The immediate conflict dramatized in this poem may be expressed most simply as the tension between temptation and loyalty. At least two years have passed since the death of Charles's mistress, and during this period he cannot have been totally deprived of female society. Opportunities to deepen casual acquaintances must have presented themselves from time to time, and now that the initial period of mourning is over, these occasions may be taken seriously. On the other hand, the dictates of conscience cannot be ignored. Beneath this obvious conflict, however, lies a deeper and more central problem concerning the poet's sense of identity.

When he wrote <u>Songe en complainte</u> Charles d'Orléans was almost forty-three years old, barely middle-aged by modern standards. But given the disparity between medieval and modern longevities, one cannot judge his age by twentieth-century criteria. Life in the late Middle Ages was an especially risky business, and a man of Charles's age could well consider himself fortunate to be still alive. It is difficult, of course, to delineate precisely the boundaries of old age in terms of the medieval concept of life, but one may say with fair assurance that the average man of forty-three felt closer to death then than he would today. Yet, although he feels closer to Old Age than Youth, the poet cannot squarely situate himself in the domain of either one. Here arises the basic conflict. The decision of whether or not to attempt a new relationship with another woman hinges entirely upon the resolution of this dilemma. The appearance of <u>Aage</u> at the outset of the poem, like Villon's mention of his age in the first verse of the <u>Testament</u>, indicates a preoccupation with time, as well as the poet's need to locate his true position in the trajectory of his life.

According to the old man of the dream, to abandon

Love automatically entails the acceptance of Old Age as
a new master. The argument is valid, however, only
insofar as it applies to a man of fairly advanced age.
Clearly, a younger man would not be compelled by either
reason or honor to renounce his quest for love. The
poet's state of agitation and indecision upon waking
from the dream proves that a part of his psyche is
unwilling to yield to the advice of <u>Aage</u>.

Were these choices to be accepted as the only
options, the poem would have to end on a note of shame
or acquiescence. Instead a third course is discovered.
After taking reluctant leave of <u>Amours</u>, the poet
directs <u>Confort</u> to lead him to the manor of <u>Non-
chaloir</u>; in our interpretation of this decision lies a
key to the meaning of the poem's conclusion. What are
we to make of this place of retreat which will serve as
the poet's permanent dwelling? It is important to
note, first of all, that <u>Nonchaloir</u> is described as a
manor and not a monastery, that favorite destination of
disillusioned courtly lovers. This fact rules out the
ascetic renunciation of worldly pleasures. Yet, like a
monastery, the manor offers this disheartened traveler
a refuge from the weariness of daily cares. Filled
with childhood memories, it further offers him the
chance to return to the innocence and tranquillity of
his earliest years.

The return to <u>Nonchaloir</u> is clearly intended to be
taken as a statement of personal philosophy. The word,
originally used to indicate a lack of heat or ardor,
had by the fifteenth century gathered a cluster of mean-
ings similar to those associated with our derivative,
"nonchalance." By choosing to dwell in <u>Nonchaloir</u>,
the poet is adopting a position that the existential-
ists might call <u>non engagé</u>. After repeatedly experi-
encing the sorrow of personal attachments brutally and
unexpectedly severed, and overcome by a cumulative weariness, Charles is now ready for a long-needed rest. To
pursue a new amorous relationship would only invite
more pain and disillusionment. What he does not define
is the scope of his newly adopted attitude of indifference. Does the apathy extend beyond love to other
areas of his life? Has he opted for moral and spiritual laxity as a solution to the increasing burden of solitude? So general an application of <u>Nonchaloir</u> does
not appear to be supported by the courtly context of
the <u>Songe</u>. But appearing, as it does, in a poem

fraught with broad philosophical implications, the term may cover ground outside the perimeters of courtly ideology, and a wider interpretation should not therefore be summarily dismissed.

With the decision to live in <u>Nonchaloir</u> and share the company of his obliging host, <u>Passe Temps</u>, the poet finally solves the conflict concerning age. Too old to throw himself back into the service of his present lord, too young to accept Old Age as a new master, he will simply free himself altogether from servitude. <u>Passe Temps</u>, not a superior but a companion, will fill the gap created by the absence of love. Diversion will buy the poet time. The concluding section of the narrative evidences feelings of serenity and contentment brought about by the successful resolution of the original dilemma. By replacing the quest for love with the quest for amusement, the poet returns to childlike values; this explains the childhood memories associated with <u>Nonchaloir</u>. Secure within the artificial world of the game, he is temporarily sheltered from the threat of uncontrollable forces. In the simplicity and innocence of play he finds reprieve from the endless entanglements of emotional commitment.

Buoyed by a resurgence of vitality, the poet reaffirms his separation from Old Age:

> Mais, Dieu merci, loing suis da sa puissance,
> Presentement je ne la crains en riens,
> (1:117)

> (But, thank God, I am far from her reach,
> At present I have no fear of her,)

From old age he has returned to childhood, then back to mature adulthood. From this vantage point he confronts <u>Vieillesse</u>, but only from a safe distance. Having finally situated himself in the course of his life, he ends by situating himself very precisely within a broader temporal context: "Written this third day of November toward the evening." The awareness of the present moment, integrating personal and historical time, brings the dream to an end.

Legalistic Aspects of the <u>Songe</u>

Charles's longest poem is significant not only as an

illumination of a personal drama, but also as an example of the expanding lexical range of fifteenth-century courtly poetry. One could hardly find a more courtly topic than the subject of this work which, taken at face value, may be reduced to the question: "What are the limits of my loyalty to love?" Admittedly, Charles draws heavily upon conventional stores of feudalistic imagery to represent the problem in figurative terms, but he also borrows from a lexicon not traditionally associated with the courtly lyric.

The requeste presented to Love contains numerous examples of legalistic language characteristic of the formal style used in laws, deeds, wills, and other legal documents of the period:

> Supplie presentement...
> >   (1:105)

> (Presently solicits...)

> Qu'il vous plaise regarder
>   Et passer
> Ceste requeste presente
> >   (1:105)

> (That it please you to examine
>   And approve
> The present petition)

> Afin que le suppliant
>   Cy devant
> Nommé...
> >   (1:107)

> (In order that the forenamed plaintiff...)

Specimens of the same style found in Love's answering quittance are reminiscent of administrative documents such as those issued by Charles's officers and signed by his own hand:

> Outre plus, faisons assavoir,
> Et certiffions, pour tout voir...
> >   (1:113)

> (Moreover, we make known

> And certify as true...)
>
> En tesmoing de ce avons mis
> Nostre seel, plaqué et assis
> En ceste presente quittance,
> Escripte par nostre ordonnance.
>   (1:113)
>
> (In witness of which we have affixed
> Our seal, properly placed,
> To this letter of exemption,
> Written under our order.)

Incorporated into the poem we find legal concepts as well as language. The poet's request to be released from Love's service has all the appearances of a carefully constructed legal case. The parlement clearly functions as a judiciary body in confirming Love's ruling. The requeste and quittance serve as documentary evidence further conferring an official status on the final verdict.

It is not surprising that Charles should be well acquainted with the complexities of legal jargon. A large part of his executive duties consisted of reading and approving documents drawn up by his secretaries and covering a wide range of legal transactions. This administrative function, as mentioned, continued to be exercised via correspondence for the duration of his exile. What is interesting, however, is that he would choose to transfer a relatively mundane aspect of his daily life into the intimate realm of poetry. This is, to be sure, not the first incursion of the legal vocation into medieval French literature. The growing importance of the profession in the fourteenth and fifteenth centuries is demonstrated by the appearance of the lawyer as a stock character of the farce, and the proliferation of legalistic terminology in prose works, especially in the chronicles.

Of the various genres, lyric poetry had shown the most stubborn resistance to the intrusion of this and other "worldly" influences so completely alien to the courtly tradition. The contamination of courtly language by lexical elements hitherto excluded from the lyric modes indicates the occurrence of two interrelated phenomena. First, historical changes were continually modifying the existing social order. Literature,

as a cultural product, was also constantly changing in
response to the society's evolving self-concept. The
collapse of the feudal structure, for example, can be
seen reflected in the gradual deterioration of feudal
values increasingly evident in later medieval literature. At the same time, literary genres, like those of
our own time, were developing according to mysterious
inner dynamics which the literary historian can never
fully grasp. As a result of this natural process of
evolution, various types of literature became receptive
at different moments to external influences to which
they had previously been immune. French lyric poetry
of the fifteenth century, having undergone certain
"organic" changes, was now susceptible to an infiltra-
tion that would ultimately bring great enrichment to
the genre.

Charles d'Orléans was not the first poet to inte-
grate courtly and non-courtly expression, but his synthesis of the two in Songe en complainte is by far
one of the most interesting attempts. His task is
facilitated by the ease with which courtly material
lends itself to legalistic treatment. Chrétien de
Troyes and Thomas d'Angleterre rely greatly on the
rhetoric of debate to sustain their long-winded mono-
logues on love. In the jeux-partis, poems constructed in the form of a debate, the trouvères attack questions concerning love with the relish of theologians
arguing a particularly thorny problem of textual interpretation. The puys, poetry competitions begun in
the thirteenth century, were organized on a judicial
model and carried out with all the formality of legal
proceedings (2). Compared with these subtle similarities, however, Charles's use of legal analogies in
Songe en complainte is unusually explicit. The poem
marks a turning point not only in the poet's life but
in his style as well. It is one of the earliest signs
of a new voice, one which will incorporate imaginative
metaphorical language into a traditional mode of poetic
discourse. The Songe is the work of a poet approaching his maturity.

Chapter Six
The Songs
Circumstances of Composition

At some point during his residence in England, probably after Bonne's death, Charles composed a series of eighty-nine songs which express his feelings for a young lady referred to simply as Beauté. These pieces, closely conforming to the structure of the rondeau (to be described in a later chapter), appear in the original manuscript between blocks of space reserved for transcription of the musical accompaniment. This score, whether to have been provided by the duke himself or by a professional musician, never materialized.

Despite all efforts to identify the lady addressed in these songs, we know practically nothing about her. That Charles did in fact become infatuated with an English lady is, however, virtually certain (1). In one of the pieces Charles speaks of sending the lady a song, and the manuscript contains a copy of one sent to him, proving Beauté's ability to communicate in French. (Two of his songs, incidentally, are written in English.) Charles's fondness for poetic messages is well known, and the majority of these songs are clearly intended for personal communication. Frequent reference to private and public meetings, plans for future encounters, allusions to words and kisses exchanged, all suggest that the duke's advances were met with tolerance if not encouragement. Judging from textual evidence, we may say that the lady was considerably younger than her admirer, of noble birth, and if the poet is to be believed, a person of exceptional grace, poise, and beauty.

Given the obvious biographical relevance of these poems, it is surprising that they have attracted such scant attention. Critical studies of Charles's poetry tend either to treat the songs superficially, lump them indiscriminately with work of an earlier or later period, or else omit them altogether. This reluctance to consider the songs as a body of poetry worthy of careful scrutiny stems mainly from their problematic na-

ture. Are they to be treated as poems or songs? To
whom were they written? And where do they fit into the
evolution of Charles's poetic personality? Are these
serious or frivolous pieces? To be sure, the songs
raise a number of perplexing questions. At the same
time, they reveal a very human side of the poet, and
there is something captivating about the little dramas
they contain.

Charles's songs lack the lofty and spiritually uplifting qualities of Petrarch's sonnets for Laura,
undoubtedly the most famous of late medieval love
poems. Nor do they possess the literary self-conscious-
ness of some of Ronsard's love sonnets. They are for
the most part unelaborated statements of feeling, written primarily, it would seem, to convey an open or
veiled message to the lady. It is in this spirit that
they should be read. Like his love ballads, these are
poems with a mission. One may reasonably question
whether all of the love sonnets of Petrarch and Ronsard
were written with no larger an audience in mind than
that of a single lady. Charles's songs, on the other
hand, demonstrate a greater concern for communication
than for their durability as works of art. This emphasis is at the same time their attraction and their
weakness.

The Relationship

While Charles's ballads tend to be deeply introspective, bearing constant witness to the poet's isolation
and strong yearning for reunion with his loved one, the
center of attention now shifts dramatically. With an
actively pursued goal to prevent him from slipping into
the abyss of the self, Charles's thoughts turn to
Beauté and to the relationship he is building with
her. His ardent desire to see this relationship deepen
informs these poems with an almost adolescent enthusiasm and spontaneity. Their impetuous cadence and
starkness of content contrast sharply with the measured
rhythm and highly figurative language of the ballads,
and argue eloquently for the authenticity of Charles's
feelings. They give the impression of an overwhelming
emotion, and there often seems to be a sense of urgency
about their composition. These are not the most sophisticated of his compositions, but, like the ballads
on the death of his lady, they are among the most
emotionally charged.

From the songs, scattered bits of information may be loosely pieced together. What emerges is not a neatly ordered chronological narration, but rather a collection of thoughts, perceptions, occasional concrete data, all of which indicate an exchange of affection or, at the very least, a mutual feeling of deep respect. In a song purportedly written two days after Charles's first encounter with Beauté he declares himself hopelessly in love. The poet, according to his own confession, has made a determined effort to resist the feminine charms surrounding him and now can prevail no longer. He is overwhelmed by the graciousness and beauty of this particular lady, seduced by the way she talks, laughs, dances, and sings. In a flattering appraisal he pictures her without French or English rival. Continuing in this hyperbolic vein, he compares her presence to the sudden and dazzling appearance of the sun. Nor is he the only one affected:

> Il fait perdre la contenance
> A toutes gens, jeunes et vielz;
> N'il n'est eclipse, se m'aist Dieux,
> Qui de l'obscurcir ait puissance;
> (1:238)

> (It [this sun] causes all people,
> Young and old, to lose countenance;
> Nor is there an eclipse, so help me God,
> Capable of obscuring it;)

This sort of inflated praise as well as the undivided attention it lavishes upon its object are not typically found in the ballads, far more self-centered by comparison.

Behind Charles and Beauté lurk shadowy figures whose identity is never disclosed, but whose sole purpose, it seems, is to intrude upon the privacy the poet so desires. They may be other male admirers, members of the lady's entourage, or some other third party determined to keep the burgeoning romance from developing too far. In addition to closely observing Charles and his young lady friend when they are together, they see to it that their encounters are kept to a minimum. But instead of acting as a deterrent, forced separation only strengthens the poet's desire:

> Ou regard de voz beaulz doulx yeulx,

> Dont loing suis par les envieux,
> Me souhaide si tressouvent
> Que mon penser est seulement
> En vostre gent corps gracieux.
>   (1:209)

> (In the look of your beautiful sweet eyes,
> From which I am far because of the envious
>   ones,
> I wish myself so very often
> That my thought is on nothing else
> But your lovely gracious body.)

In an operation with which we are by now familiar, the distance maintained by physical barriers is closed by means of memory and imagination. Beginning with the lady's gaze, the poet ends with his own, as he inwardly contemplates her image. The transition occurs with the pivotal verb souhaide placed almost precisely in the middle of the stanza, thus contributing to the impression of symmetry. In the contact between the woman's body and the poet's thought, that most intimate facet of his being, a subtle sensuality may be perceived, heightened by the physical separation which prevents more substantial contact from taking place.

Her image, Charles says, fills his waking and sleeping hours:

> En songe, souhaid et pensee,
> Vous voy chascun jour de sepmaine,
> Combien qu'estes de moy loingtaine,
> Belle, tresloyaumment amee.
>   (1:220)

> (In dream, wish, and thought,
> I see you every day of the week,
> Although you are far from me,
> Beautiful lady, so loyally loved.)

The effect of her presence (and absence) is easy enough to gauge. Her attitude toward Charles, on the other hand, appears to have been subject to fluctuation. In her one recorded poem she speaks with frankness of her devotion to him, and makes it clear that her feelings extend well beyond the bounds of mere friendship. He warmly thanks her at one point for a token of affection whose nature is not specified. But in a less jubilant moment he apologizes for having angered her, although he himself seems uncertain of the reason for her displeasure. In another poem he throws himself at her mercy, saying that he has heard she is unhappy with him. This news has cost him a sleepless night, and he begs to be enlightened on the cause of his sudden disfavor.

Whatever personal conflicts may have developed in the course of this relationship, there is hardly a sour note to be found in Charles's songs. Instead a firm and joyful optimism dominates this verse. Savored memories and the thought of future meetings provide the momentum necessary to keep from falling into passivity or self-pity. Even without knowing anything about the young English lady, of how long the relationship lasted and how fully it was allowed to mature or how it finally ended, we can hardly fail to discern the authentic inspiration of the text. Charles's poetry is now controlled by the emotions it once sought to order. Hastily finishing a song in anticipation of an approaching rendezvous, he makes no effort to conceal his enthusiasm:

> Bien brief pense partir decy
> Pour m'en aler vers vous de tire;
> Loisir n'ay pas de vous escrire,
> (1:234)

> (Very soon I intend to leave here
> To go to you straightaway;
> I have no time to write to you;)

If these are not poems inspired by genuine love, they are indeed a most convincing counterfeit.

Troubadour Echoes

Of all Charles's poetry, it is his songs that come closest to the work of his most distant predecessors, the troubadours. Examples of this similarity are numerous. First, like the canzo d'amors, these pieces are written in the form of a message, a kind of versified love letter. But while the troubadours often addressed their poems to fictitious women, intending their work to be performed rather than used as a means of private

communication, this clearly is not true of Charles's
poems for his English lady. There is therefore a definite sense of intimacy about these pieces not necessarily found in troubadour poetry. For here, as in the
case of Charles's love ballads, we have in our hands a
relative rarity in medieval French lyric poetry, a
series of poems which we know to have been composed for
and destined to an actual person.

Like the canzo d'amors, these poems were written
as songs. The fact that melodies never materialized in
the form of notation does not detract from the musical
quality of this poetry. The compression of a highly
charged emotional statement into the space of some
dozen lines of verse creates an intensity, a lyricism
seldom surpassed in Charles's other work.

Another resemblance to troubadour poetry may be
found in the directness of the poetic discourse. Compelled both by the brevity of the chosen form and the
urgency of his message, Charles can no longer afford
the luxury of extended allegory and other rhetorical
devices. The ornamented language of the ballad now
yields to a stark plainness which is almost blunt by
comparison. Yet, like the confessions of love in the
canzo d'amors, the forcefulness of this bluntness is
usually tempered by the harmonious tones of its expression.

Examples of traditional courtly ideology abound.
Striking the classic pose of the martyred lover,
Charles affirms his loyalty:

> Ma dame, tant qu'il vous plaira
> De me faire mal endurer,
> Mon cueur est prest de le porter,
> Jamais ne le refusera.
>
> (1:215)

> (My lady, as long as it pleases you
> To make me suffer hurt,
> My heart is ready to bear it,
> Never will it refuse.)

As in troubadour poetry, Charles's self-styled martyrdom is made more tolerable by the hope for a much-
sought recompense. This reward is, of course, the
lady's love, and specifically any tangible proof of it
she may offer. The fulfillment of this desire, both

realized and imagined, underlies the feeling of joy so prevalent in the <u>canzo d'amors</u>, and the erotic qualities of these earliest love songs have long been recognized. Although the eroticism of Charles's songs is of a subtler nature, this series of poems displays a frank sensuality that is totally without precedent in his earlier work.

The songs are filled with encomiums of the young lady's beauty. Charles confesses that he would gladly stare at her constantly, but fears that the rumors generated by such obvious adulation might harm her reputation. His physical attraction to her reveals itself most often in the recurrent motif of the kiss. There are, he states, two kinds: those given in public as a gesture of polite greeting, and those given in secret. The lady's chaperons apparently could not have been omnipresent, for not all the kisses exchanged are of the public variety:

> Dedans mon sein, pres de mon cueur
> J'ay mussié un privé baisier
> (1:223)

> (Within my breast, near my heart
> I have hidden a private kiss)

It seems that the clandestine meetings such as the one alluded to above took place in less than ideal conditions. In one song, Charles urges his heart to quickly take the kiss his lady offers while he, the poet, stands guard.

The request for a kiss is sometimes discreet or even coy:

> Se desplaire ne vous doubtoye,
> Voulentiers je vous embleroye
> Un doulx baisier priveement,
> Et garderoye seurement
> Dedens le tresor de ma joye.
> (1:227)

> (If I did not fear displeasing you,
> Willingly would I steal from you
> A sweet kiss in private,
> And I would keep it safe
> Within the treasury of my joy.)

At other times the advance is so direct that it borders on audacity:

> Vostre bouche dit: Baisiez moy,
> Se m'est avis quant la regarde;
> (1:232)

> (Your mouth says, "Kiss me,"
> So it seems to me when I look at it;)

Kisses are also a subject of gentle teasing. The young lady is advised that if her kisses were for sale, her French suitor would buy them by the "dozen, hundred, or thousand." But, he adds, he would expect them at a lower price than that she would ask of a stranger. Another poem continues the financial or commercial analogy (a type of metaphor that will be developed in the later ballads), as the poet asserts that his lady is several kisses "indebted" to him, and warns that if she does not pay off what is owed, she will be arrested by the "officers of Love."

Among the brash and timid advances and the playful complaints are also to be found descriptions of intimacy, touching in their simplicity:

> Logies moy entre voz bras,
> Et m'envoiez doulx baisier
> (1:229)

> (Lodge me in your arms
> And send me a sweet kiss)

The verb <u>envoyer</u> undercuts the physical closeness suggested in the first verse, and gives a slightly tragic twist to what appeared at first to be an obliviously blissful scene. For the "sending" of the kiss implies some sort of distance separating poet and lady even in the intimate moment of embrace. And the fact that he seeks to be "lodged" in her arms bespeaks a realization that this, like any other lodging, is only a temporary refuge.

Only once does Charles request more than a kiss and embrace. If his lady knew the extent of his suffering, he says, she would find a way to ease the pain:

> Et le don me donneriés
> Que vous ay requis souvent,
> (1:213)

> (And you would give me the gift
> I have often asked of you,)

By ancient convention the word <u>don</u> is understood in courtly terminology to designate a woman's surrender of her body, and the context of the poet's request leaves little room for ambiguity.

These little poems, written in a wide range of tones and communicating an equally wide variety of messages, stand apart from the rest of Charles's poetic production. Here, more than in any other phase of his work, the presence of another person can be seen as the primary inspirational force. The lady of the ballads inspires by her absence rather than her presence. Ladies appear in the rondeaux as a subject of amusement more than inspiration. To be sure, the songs generally lack the depth of the ballads and the luster of the rondeaux. But they possess, on the other hand, a winning frankness of expression that endows them with a distinctive character.

Chapter Seven
The English Poetry

Of the mysteries surrounding the poetry Charles composed prior to 1440, one of the most intriguing is the question of the English poetry that some attribute to him. A manuscript of unknown origin, dating from around the middle of the fifteenth century and containing 6,531 lines of verse in which Charles d'Orléans is cited several times (in the first person) as the author, was first published in 1827 (1). It was not until 1941 that the manuscript was republished by Robert Steele, who in his introduction presented what he believed to be substantial evidence corroborating Charles's authorship (2). Steele's claim reopened the controversy over the manuscript's ultimate origin. Critical opinion has basically divided itself along geographical lines, Anglo-American scholars tending to accept the hypothesis, while their French counterparts view it with some skepticism.

The poems of the English manuscript are grouped into three general divisions which Steele entitles: "The First Sequence of Ballades," "The Banquet of Song and Dance," and "The New Fortune in Love." The first section consists of the Retinue d'amours, seventy of Charles's ballads and the Songe en complainte, all rendered in English, as well as five ballads concerning the death of the lady, which have no French equivalent. These poems, following the sequential order of the oldest and most reliable manuscript of Charles's French poetry, describe the poet's apprenticeship with Love, his devotion to the "Peerless Lady," her death, and his subsequent renunciation of love. The next section is a lyric interlude comprised of a ballad, fifty-two songs, and three carols, all based on French equivalents, as well as three ballads and forty-two songs without corresponding versions in French. This eclectic collection contains no discernible thread of continuity, and the narrative line does not resume until the third section of the work. Here we find four ballads and a complainte based on French pieces, as well as thirty-five

ballads and a lengthy allegory (616 verses) for which
no French equivalent exists. The narrative poem
relates a dream in which the poet meets Venus and
Fortune and has a vision of the lady who will become
his new love. He awakens in the presence of the lady
whom he recognizes from the dream. The remaining ballads are written to this person, whose identity is
never revealed. Taken together, the first and last of
the manuscript's three sections form a loosely structured autobiographical sequence.

Steele's hypothesis is based on a number of perceptive observations, none of which is conclusive in
itself, but which, taken cumulatively, lend a certain
credibility to his argument. First, nine poems written
in English appear in Charles's sole surviving personal
manuscript; it is generally agreed that he is the
author of all nine. Some have attributed a number of
these pieces to the English and Scottish visitors he is
known to have received at Blois (3). In any case, the
two poems that appear in his handwriting are adequate
proof of his mastery of English:

> Whan shal thow come, Glad Hope, fro the vyage?
> Thow hast taryed to long many a day.
> For all conford is put from my away
> Tyll that I her tything of thy message.
>
> (1:256)

Being fascinated by language (he experimented with
Latin poetry as well), it is only natural that the poet
would have tried his hand at English verse. Furthermore, the English chronicler Raphael Holinshed asserts
that Charles returned to France, "speaking better English than French" (4). René d'Anjou, Charles's intimate friend and a frequent visitor to Blois, states in
his Livre du Cueur d'Amours espris [Book of the heart
captured by love] that Charles's knowledge of the
language allowed him to make the acquaintance of a certain English lady with whom he fell in love. This
could well be the same lady who appears at the end of
the dream allegory.

To this evidence must be added the fact that the English and French manuscripts resemble each other in
shape, size, and arrangement of verse on the page. As
for the correctness of the language, John Fox, a noted
British medievalist, finds the verse faulty from the

standpoint of syntax and vocabulary. He believes it to
be the work of a non-native speaker with a keen ear and
considerable poetic talent, all of which point in his
opinion to Charles d'Orléans.

Tempting though the theory of Charles's authorship
may be, it does leave a number of disturbing questions
unanswered. Why, for example, does the writer of the
English ballads consistently supply envois where none
exist in the French? Another puzzling point is the
emphasis on the figures of Venus and Fortune in the
dream allegory, an emphasis lacking in the two French
allegories. The eighty-six consecutive lines devoted
to the description of Fortune are totally without parallel in Charles's narrative poems, where description
tends to be laconic and sparingly used. Finally, how
does one explain the paucity of English verse in the
personal manuscript of a poet who at one time composed
over six thousand lines in that language? There may
well exist a plausible answer to each of these questions, but the ones advanced so far have failed to con-
vince those critics who approach Steele's hypothesis
with suspicion.

In spite of the objections it has raised, the claim
of Charles's involvement in the English poetry is becoming increasingly difficult to refute. Norma Goodrich
has amply demonstrated the thematic unity that bonds
the French and English work. Others have pointed to
the stylistic unity running throughout the English
poetry, a fact which would seem to suggest a single
author for those poems with, as well as those without,
French versions. However, the question of whether the
manuscript might be the work of an unknown English
translator is still far from resolved. Sergio Cigada,
one of the most highly respected critics of Charles
d'Orléans, favors the translator hypothesis. It has
been suggested that the Earl of Suffolk, who was himself a bilingual poet, may have had a hand in the work
(5).

The fact that French versions exist for some of the
English poems but not for others only complicates the
case. And why was the manuscript left in England? One
possible explanation would be that the manuscript was
intended as a gift to the mysterious lady mentioned in
the dream allegory. This would at once resolve the
questions of why the manuscript was left behind and why
it was put into English in the first place. If one

accepts the hypothesis, it would be understandable that the last section of the work, the part specifically addressed to the poet's new lady, be composed almost entirely without the aid of a French equivalent. On the other hand, the older pieces, composed before making her acquaintance, would naturally have been written in French and later translated. This reasoning would support the argument of those who view Charles d'Orléans as the authentic creator of the English verse.

By now the complexity of the issue should be apparent. Much investigation remains to be done in this area, and a definite conclusion may never be reached. Until such time as this mystery is solved, the English poetry will remain a fascinating enigma.

Chapter Eight
Prince of the Poetic Court
The Setting

When Charles returned to France in 1440 he immersed himself in worldly concerns which left him little time for writing poetry. With the collapse of the Italian expedition and his subsequent failure to raise funds for a second attempt, Charles abandoned his role as a military leader and settled permanently in Blois. It was during this period of newly found tranquillity that he produced most of his rondeaux. In order to appreciate the distinct qualities that set this phase of his verse apart from the earlier poetic corpus, our attention must first be turned to the milieu in which the work was produced and whose influence upon the poet was so important.

Highly private in nature, the exile poetry is mainly comprised of meditations and poetic correspondence. It was not intended primarily for the public eye. A large portion of the later poetry, by contrast, was composed with a specific audience in mind, namely, the court of Blois. Many of Charles's rondeaux were written in reply to those composed by others--friends, visiting acquaintances, members of the domestic staff--or else as a challenge demanding a response from these persons. Most of the major poets of the period found their way to Blois at some point, and left behind contributions in the duke's personal album. Within his own lifetime Charles's court was to gain a reputation as one of the most dynamic centers of poetic activity in France.

Because of its central geographic location and the famous warm welcome its owner always bestowed upon traveling nobility, the castle of Blois under Charles d'Orléans received its share of important guests. In the long list of visitors who were lodged at least once in Blois we find such distinguished names as Jean, Duke of Alençon; Jean, Duke of Bourbon; Philippe of Burgundy and his wife, Isabelle; Charles de Nevers (a Burgundian prince); and Charles d'Orléans's good friend, René d'Anjou, who preferred the title King of Sicily. The entourage of these aristocratic travelers occasionally included writers of considerable talent whose poetic contributions, as well as those of their less skilled superiors, were solicited for Charles's collection.

The festivities prompted by the arrival of each of these honored guests typify the spirit of jubilation that immediately followed the Hundred Years' War. Except for scattered and relatively minor eruptions of violence, the civil strife which had torn the country for generations was now rapidly subsiding. Life could finally return to some semblance of normality. During holidays and the stays of visiting dignitaries, the periods richest in communally centered poetic activity, the prevailing atmosphere at Blois was one of levity, if not pure frivolity.

Charles's court was hardly among the most sumptuous in France, nor did he attempt to rival the extravagance of his wealthier peers. His material tastes, like his literary aesthetics, were dominated by a strong sense of proportion. Still Blois was by no means a picture of austerity. In 1446 he had the western wing of the castle renovated in order to accommodate more comfortably court visitors and attendants. The inner walls were hung with tapestries in typical medieval fashion, and we are told that the chapel contained an especially beautiful gold relief fastened to the wall with silver nails. The ledger of expenses shows that the acquisition of handsomely bound books accounted for an appreciable portion of household expenditures. With the revenue generated by the salt tax, collected from his lands as a privilege accorded by Charles VII in 1443, Charles was able to maintain an appropriately elegant, though not lavish, standard of living. Servants and various objects of art imported from Asti reminded guests of their host's Italian descent. Whatever Blois lacked in ostentation it made up in refinement.

During the period when it served as Charles's main place of residence, the fame of Blois was based not only on its hospitality but also on the type of entertainment one was sure to find there. Charles had always been an avid game player, and, as a court tends to emulate the tastes of the one who presides over it, Blois became known for its emphasis on cultivated diversion. Chess and an early form of backgammon, two of Charles's favorite pastimes, were constantly being played. The most challenging and artistically refined form of recreation, however, were the poetry contests organized by the duke himself.

Although appearing to be competitive in nature (participants were required to compose from a common point of departure, sometimes a selected proverb), the "contest" was in all likelihood limited to vying for praise rather than officially awarded recognition. Rather than a competition, the event was instead a means of earning or sustaining membership in a kind of male club. Except for the virtual exclusion of women (whose recorded contributions are so few as to be practically insignificant), this poetic fraternity exhibited surprisingly democratic tendencies. Unlike contemporary chivalric orders, admission into the privileged circle was not limited to the social elite, but was also granted in recognition of wit and genuine talent regardless of origin. We find, therefore, poems by dukes and servants mixed indiscriminately in the same album.

Many of the contributions to the collection, particularly those written by its owner, are filled with bantering remarks directed toward certain members of the duke's literary coterie. Although unable to appreciate all the nuances of these highly personal (and therefore often obscure) allusions, we can still easily grasp their intent. In one such reference Charles indulges in a little good-natured fun at the expense of his young friend, Jean II, Duke of Bourbon, whose delicate digestion was evidently well known at Blois:

> Helas! et qui ne l'aymeroit,
> De Bourbon, le droit heritier,
> Qui a l'estomac de papier
> Et aura la goute de droit!
>   (2:374)

> (Alas! and who would not like
> The rightful heir of Bourbon,
> Who has a paper stomach
> And will have gout by right of inheritance.)

One can imagine that the teasing remark was accepted by the young duke in the same spirit in which it was written. Many such polished poetic barbs were exchanged among the members of Charles's circle, but rarely if ever with any trace of malice. Apparently the atmosphere at Blois, unlike that of many other courts, was not one to foster jealousy and paranoia.

Although a large number of his later poems yield no clues to the circumstances of their composition, we know that many, if not all, were destined for a specific audience, and one, moreover, with which the poet was intimately acquainted. This small and heterogeneous body (the phrase "captive audience" comes to mind, but carries pejorative connotations which cannot be fairly applied here) warrants scrutiny for several reasons. An understanding of the literary ambience of Blois necessitates at least a rudimentary acquaintance with the visitors and court residents who contributed to its reputation. Also, since a significant number of Charles's poems were composed in conjunction with pieces of different authorship but similar theme and tone, a glance at the identities of these "partners" may help to set this poetic interplay in its proper perspective.

One of our most important sources of information concerning the literary circle at Blois is, of course, Charles's personal manuscript (1). This book served a social as well as a litereay purpose, functioning as a kind of guest register in which honored visitors were asked to leave a poem as a memento of their stay in Blois. The contributors to the album fall into three basic categories: visiting nobility, professional writers, and members of the duke's entourage. Although their relations with Charles d'Orléans may be of some historical interest, the aristocratic contributors left few pieces of literary merit. Their poems were solicited merely out of politeness, and the resulting efforts, mostly mediocre, were probably included in the collection for their value as memorabilia rather than for their artistic character. With two notable exceptions, the contribution of such visitors was limited to one or two poems apiece. The names of René d'Anjou and Jean II of Bourbon (the duke's junior by thirty-three years) appear frequently throughout the album. Charles is known to have been fond of both, and, whether out of a desire to please or genuine interest, they actively collaborated in various exchanges and contests (2).

Socially prominent visitors sometimes brought in their company men who made their living by writing. Well educated and well traveled, they generally served in a secretarial or advisory capacity to their aristo-

cratic employers. All came with established reputa-
tions as poets, and one can easily imagine the relish
with which they welcomed the opportunity to display
their talents at Blois. Among these contributors we
find the names of some of the most important French
writers of the fifteenth century: Georges Chastellain,
advisor to Philippe the Good, and later, official chronicler of the House of Burgundy; Olivier de la Marche,
author of another well-known set of memoirs; Jean
Meschinot, a Breton poet; and Vaillant (Pierre
Chastellain), harp player and court poet of René
d'Anjou. To this list must be added the name of a
writer little known in his day but whose poetry would
eventually thrust almost all other fifteenth-century
poets into obscurity. The <u>povre Villon</u>, as he liked
to call himself, is known to have passed through Blois
at least once during his mysterious wanderings subsequent to the Navarre affair of 1456. It must be recognized, however, that the contributions of these
writers, although clearly superior to the amateurish
efforts of Charles's other collaborators, form no more
than a small portion of the "solicited" poetry in the
duke's manuscript.

The majority of those who participated in the poetic
contests were not guests, but residents of the court,
by and large young men from respected families who had
been selected to serve as squires or attendants while
awaiting more prestigious and lucrative positions.
Often assigned to easy duties which they were expected
to discharge only in a perfunctory manner, these spirit-
ed young gentlemen had no trouble finding ample time
for amusement. For Charles their company provided a
valued source of companionship and entertainment. Some
gained favor with the duke as chess partners as well as
participants in the poetry competitions. A few, such
as Benoist Damien and Gille des Ormes, were to become
especially dear to Charles. Both show a poetic talent
which can only have stood them in good stead at Blois.
To these and others Charles gave numerous expensive
gifts betokening a natural generosity and a feeling of
genuine affection.

As we read through the many lighthearted poetic exchanges recorded in Charles's manuscript we readily
sense a warmth and spirit of camaraderie beneath the

banter, a cheerful familiarity from which neither age nor social rank exclude the duke. On one occasion, Charles, no doubt much to the delight of his protegés, gently chides a certain Fredet for neglecting his former friends now that he is married (3). On another, he playfully ridicules the sexual misadventure of his friend and secretary, Etienne Le Gout, borrowing terms from Latin grammar to dignify the unflattering episode:

> De fenestre assez superlative
> A fait un sault portant coups en passif,
> (2:301)

> (From a rather superlative window
> He took a leap carrying blows in the passive,)

Charles clearly enjoyed the company of his entourage. In the relationship of the aging duke, still without a son, to his young companions there is something benevolent and even paternal.

Charles's sovereignty over the court of Blois extended also into the sphere of poetic activity where he was rightfully regarded as the undisputed master. His influence is evident throughout the album; also evident is the gap between authentic inspiration and blind imitation. In addition to his literary fame, Charles was also esteemed as a man well experienced in the art of love. Whether this reputation was deserved or not, he made no effort to disavow it. On the contrary, he appears to have cultivated the image, freely distributing cynical advice to novice lovers:

> Que voulez vous que plus vous die,
> Jeunes assotez amoureux?
> Par Dieu, j'ay esté l'un de ceulx
> Qui ont eu vostre maladie!
> (2:323)

> (What more do you want me to say,
> Young infatuated lovers?
> By God, I have been one of those
> Who have had your sickness.)

As will be presently seen, the language, tone, and

themes of the post-exile poetry mark a radical departure from those of the earlier period. This dramatic
shift may be ascribed to three basic factors: age, environment, and audience. Of these, the last may be the
most significant.

Blois and Its Games

The most influential artistic milieu of fifteenth-
century France was located not in Touraine or Ile-de-
France but in Burgundy. With the court of the Valois
dukes as its hub, the Burgundian school of art was without rival in France. Practically every musician of the
period, Guillaume Dufay being the most famous, had some
connection with the Burgundian court. In the sphere of
literature, and especially poetry, Burgundy's influence
was more limited. Her poets, Georges Chastellain, Jean
Molinet, and others preferred the highly ornate rhetorical style to straightforward lyric simplicity. Their
primary contribution was to lay the groundwork for the
grands rhétoriqueurs who would gain popularity
toward the end of the century. The course of lyric
poetry, unlike the evolutionary track of the other
arts, does not run through Burgundy.
The privileged status of poetry at Blois earned the
court its justly deserved reputation as a haven for
poets. Here men of much or little talent, great or
small reputation, could be assured of a receptive audience. But the poetic activity that thrived at Blois
was not totally unstructured. Under the aegis of
Charles's patronage it took on a definite form and character. Not only did he encourage promising poets and
organize competitions, but he also provided an example
on which they could model their own verse, always establishing the form and tone which would be adopted for
any given series of poems. Daniel Poirion refers to
these communal creations as a sort of jeu poétique,
and the exercise does in fact have all the appearances
of a highly sophisticated verbal game (4). One "player" sets in motion an image that is then picked up by
his "opponent" and returned with a personal twist that
gives the poem a stamp of individuality.
It would be a mistake, however, to assume that all
of Charles's later poetry is rendered superficial by a
gamelike quality. First of all, not every poem he composed during this period was written in connection with

poems of other authorship. A number of pieces, although probably intended for public display, are characterized by a pensiveness and solemnity reminiscent of his earlier ballads. Second, the often playful nature of his verse has the creative effect of loosening some of the strictures imposed upon lyric poetry by centuries of tradition. Always working within the bounds of conventional forms, mainly the ballad and the rondeau, Charles allows himself considerable linguistic and thematic latitude that gives many of his poems a decidedly unconventional nature. Furthermore, as Villon was to prove, semantic playfulness and incisive observation need not be incompatible. Like Villon, whose verbal acrobatics are more daring, Charles uses word tricks to test the intellectual and aesthetic potentialities of poetic language.

Clearly, the role of milieu in the work of Charles d'Orléans cannot be neglected. Just as the pomp, splendor, and sense of self-importance of the Burgundian court inspired an oratorical and somewhat grandiose strain of poetry, the effect of the festive atmosphere of Blois with its passion for refined amusement can be seen in the verse of the poet-prince and those who wrote under his influence. However, in this case the milieu itself was the creation of the poet. For what was Blois with all its Italianate sophistication and elegance, polished cultivation and wealth of self-sustaining courtly recreation, if not the material projection of the passions and ideals of the man who presided over it?

Chapter Nine
The Later Ballads

In the last twenty-four years of his life Charles
d'Orléans composed and recorded 344 rondeaux as op-
posed to only twenty-eight ballads. Although he clearly found the more compact and musical genre better suited to his taste, he continued to rely on the ballad
form when his thought required an ampler means of
expression. Contained in these pieces are patterns
woven of both old and new thematic threads. Negative
aspects of the poet's existence surface frequently:
sickness, old age, thoughts on mortality. A cynical
tone dominates this poetry, but it is a cynicism tempered with wit and humor more often than bitterness.

Old Age

The specter of Old Age which appeared in the Songe
en complainte has now become one of the poet's most
constant companions. Aging and its side-effects--weak-
ness, sickness, fatigue--emerge in fact as the central
preoccupation of the later ballads. The manner chosen
to portray the aging process varies with the poet's
mood, now peevish, now stoic. Striking a pose that
brings to mind the pathetic figure of Don Quijote mount-
ed on his broken steed, Charles describes himself:

> Portant harnoys rouillé de Nonchaloir,
> Sus montre foulee de Foiblesse,
> Mal abillé de Desireus Vouloir,
> On m'a croizé, aux montres de Liesse,
> Comme cassé des gaiges de Jeunesse.
> Je ne congnois ou je puisse servir;
> L'arriereban a fait crier Vieillesse.
> Las! fauldra il son soudart devenir?
> (1:168)

> (Wearing armor rusted by Indifference,
> On a mount exhausted by Weakness,
> Ill clad with Desirous Will,

I have been given the cross in the review of
  Happiness*
As one deprived of the wages of Youth.
I do not know where I can serve;
Old Age has had the summons called.
Alas! Shall I have to become her soldier?)

*A cross placed before the names of soldiers no
longer able to serve.

The rusted armor mentioned in the opening verse, when
seen as an extension of the soldier's body, symbolizes
the corrosive effect of time upon the poet's physical
and spiritual being. Having sustained numerous wounds
in Love's service, the weary veteran is now about to
change commanders. Military imagery in the earlier
ballads, although not uncommon, is generally restricted
to a few standard schemes. These follow conventional
lines (e.g., the arrow of Love) or involve some kind of
unelaborated architectural motif (e.g., the fortress of
the heart). In this particular poem, using a technique
seen frequently in the later ballads, Charles sustains
and expands his metaphor. The image is not only
fleshed out beyond its skeletal form but also "modern-
ized." Croizé, montres, cassé de gaiges, and
arriereban are all technical terms associated with
fifteenth-century military administration, terms completely foreign to the courtly vocabulary favored by
the poet in his earlier ballads.

The sense of impotence implied in the preceding passage is occasionally made explicit:

Desarmé suis, car pieça mon harnaiz
Je le vendy, par le conseil d'Oiseuse,
Comme lassé de la guerre amoureuse.
                              (1:171)

(I am disarmed, for long ago
I sold my weapon, on the advice of Idleness,
As one weary of the war of love.)

The term harnaiz (a variant of harnoys) translates
as "weapon" or "tool" as well as "armor," and is used
in the plural to designate the male genitals. Here
then the metaphorical weaponry of love is endowed with
an unmistakable phallic signification. Courtly tradi-

tion is again remodeled in highly uncourtly fashion.

When not disposed to joke about the aging process, the poet often protests against its injustice:

> Mon cueur vous adjourne, Viellesse,
> Par Droit, huissier de parlement,
> Devant Raison qui est maistresse
> Et juge de vray jugement.
> Depuis que le gouvernement
> Avez eu de luy et de moy,
> Vous nous avez, par tirennye,
> Mis es mains de Merencolie
> Sans savoir la cause pourquoy.
>   (1:184)

> (My heart summons you to trial, Old Age,
> By Right, bailiff of the court,
> Before Reason who is mistress
> And judge of true judgment.
> Ever since you have had government
> Over him [my heart] and me,
> You have, with tyranny,
> Put us into the hands of Melancholy
> Without our knowing why.)

Using legal analogies (adjourne, huissier de parlement, juge) to lodge his complaint, Charles continues the pattern already begun in the Songe en complainte. In a futile but touchingly human impulse, the aging poet challenges Old Age to answer to reason, who figures prominently in the later ballads. It is important to understand the plaintiff's cause for bringing suit. His quarrel with the defendant is based not on her supremacy over him, a fact he willingly accepts, but on the way she has abused her authority. Her crime is to have perfidiously surrendered the poet and his heart to Melancholy. Charles proceeds to plead his case eloquently, with Old Age remaining all the while shamefully mute.

Protest is sometimes replaced by stoic resignation. In a less agitated moment the poet is able to take a more enlightened view of his condition:

> Prenant en gré ceste rudesse,
> Le mal d'aultruy conpare au myen;
> Lors me tance Dame Sagesse,

> Adonques en moy je revien,
> Et croy de tout le conseil sien
> Qui est en ce plain de droiture,
> Puis que c'est le cours de nature.
>   (1:183)

> (Taking this rudeness in stride,
> I compare the pain of others to my own;
> Then Lady Wisdom scolds me,
> Then I return into myself,
> And totally believe her advice,
> Which in this respect is full of virtue,
> Since this is the course of nature.)

While Reason may be the ultimate arbiter, she can do no more than point an accusing finger. It is to Lady Wisdom that the poet turns for the consolation that Reason fails to provide. For wisdom counsels the poet to accept that which reason cannot explain. In a rare moment of freedom he briefly escapes the confines of the self and views his own plight against that of others. The ambiguity of the second verse opens two possible avenues of interpretation. Either he becomes cognizant of the affliction of those physically worse off than himself, or else he realizes that a certain degree of suffering is an inherent part of the human condition. Each view may be equally well interpreted as having either Christian or Stoic underpinnings.

In such a moment of uncertainty, face to face with old age and the threat of death, one would expect a man of the fervently pious fifteenth century to turn to his religion. Yet the poetry of Charles d'Orléans, in later as well as earlier periods of emotional unrest, remains remarkably secular. Parenthetical remarks such as se Dieu plaist ("if it please God") and par Dieu ("by God") do occur frequently, but these were commonplace in medieval speech and do not constitute evidence of sustained reflection. It would be inaccurate, however, to make any inference about Charles's spiritual convictions solely on the basis of his poetry. All biographical indications depict a man of unquestionable piety. We know, for example, that religious works accounted for a large portion of his library at Blois. The only valid conclusion which may be drawn is that Charles did not consider his poetry as a means well suited to the expression of religious sentiment.

The essence of Lady Wisdom's advice is contained in
the refrain: "puis que c'est le cours de nature."
Nature is mentioned by name only three times in all the
ballads. (The nature motif, as will be shown in chapter ten, occurs more frequently in the rondeaux.) Wisdom counsels the poet not to resist the inevitable
changes brought on by the cycles of life. The word
cours offers a rich variety of readings. It may
designate a road or path, a meaning retained in the
English derivative. In this case the poet would be
invited to follow a predestined course, another in a
series of étapes or stages of the journey. The term
also describes the running motion of water, especially
the movement of a river. Taken in this manner, the
cours de nature is the flow of the life-force through
all living beings. By existing in harmony with this
natural flow, and thus losing any sense of separation,
the poet may relieve himself of his burden of anxiety.
But the most interesting interpretation and the one
least evident to the modern reader is based on a game
analogy. In chess a cours means a "move," and is so
used elsewhere in the ballads. What Wisdom may be saying is "It's Nature's move." Having played his side to
the best of his ability, Charles must now yield control
of the game to his opponent while awaiting his turn.
The picture of this veteran player facing his unbeat-
able adversary across a chessboard is one by which the
poet would surely have liked to be remembered.

Sickness

Among the preoccupations reflected in Charles's second cycle of ballads, one of the most frequent is the
subject of his declining health. In his later years
the duke suffered from a variety of minor but annoying
ailments. Having developed gout, and impairments of
hearing and vision, he understandably tended to dwell
on the state of his body as well as that of his mind.
Suffering, depicted in the earlier poetry as a purely
mental phenomenon, now also takes on a physical dimension. Discomfort formerly pictured in nebulously
abstract language now finds expression in more rigorously analytical terms, such as those used by this lady in
describing her suitor's malady:

>"Il ne fault ja vostre pousse taster;
>Fievre n'avez que de merencolie,
>Vostre orine ne aussi regarder:
>Tost se garist legiere maladie."
>
>   (1:167)

>(It's hardly necessary to feel your pulse;
>The only fever you have is that of melancholy.
>Nor is it necessary to examine your urine:
>A minor illness is quickly remedied.)

The poet claims to have overheard these words, but his self-effacement is no more than a pretext for using the lady as a mouthpiece. Here again we hear the cynical veteran of Love's campaigns addressing his foolish and easily infatuated young companions. The sickness of love, that vaguest of all malaises and favorite courtly conceit, is taken literally here. The elevated style traditionally associated with this metaphor is consequently undercut by talk of urine, pulse, and fever.

The usage of merencolie deserves a brief comment. We find this key word frequently applied in the later poetry to the poet's state of mind. "Melancholy" translates only one aspect of the word. It may also signify bad humor, irritability, or what, using a clinical term, we might call a case of very mild depression. The word should be differentiated from tristesse ("sadness"), with which it is not necessarily synonymous. In characterizing his life as one often dominated by merencolie the poet is not claiming (as some have mistakenly asserted) to be subject to frequent bouts of intense dejection. Increased irascibility was thought at that time to result from an excess of melancholy or black bile, one of the four humors of the body. The term therefore signifies a physical as much as a mental condition.

The elaborated version of the sickness of love recurs in various forms. It is presented in one instance as a contagious air particularly dangerous during the winter:

>Aussi en yver le pluieux,
>Qui vens et broillars fait lever,
>L'air d'Amour epidimieux

> Souvent par my se vient bouter;
> (1:151)

> (Thus in rainy winter,
> Which raises wind and fog,
> The infectious air of Love
> Often makes an invasion;)

The implication is that the forced confinement brought on by inclement weather makes people especially susceptible to love, possibly due to an excess of idle time. But Charles's most extended treatment of illness is found in a ballad written perhaps with his personal physician, Jehan Caillau, in mind:

> Yeulx rougis, plains de piteux pleurs,
> Fourcelle d'espoir reffroidie,
> Teste enrumée de douleurs,
> Et troublee de frenesie,
> Corps perclus sans plaisance lie,
> Cueur du tout pausmé en rigueurs,
> Voy souvent avoir a plusieurs
> Par le vent de Merencolie.
> (1:172)

> (Red eyes, full of tears,
> Chest chilled of hope,
> Head congested with sorrows,
> And deranged by frenzy,
> Body immobilized without gay pleasure,
> Heart completely swooned in suffering,
> This I often see befall many people
> Because of the wind of Melancholy.)

The plusieurs targeted by the poem are again the lovesick young men whom the poet delights in ridiculing. Their "illness" is described by pairing in six consecutive instances a medical term or phrase with a word suggesting an emotional reaction. This medical/affective juxtaposition is reinforced by the dual meaning of the last word in the refrain. The ballad continues in the same vein, including dropsy, migraines, colic, gout, and kidney stones within its catalog of bodily ailments. Charles, as we know from the large number of medical treatises in his library, was well versed in pathological disorders.

   In a different context this interest in disease

might be construed as evidence of a morbid outlook. But in almost every case the most graphic imagery is applied to the amorphous "sickness of love" rather than to the poet's state of health. Used in this manner, the technique attempts to deflate courtly love of some of its esoteric mystery, and is calculated to inspire humor rather than pity.

Mortality

The late medieval mentality, as Huizinga has shown, was one deeply preoccupied if not haunted by the idea of mortality. Somber thoughts concerning the brevity and fragility of human existence intrude into practically every realm of artistic expression. In the earlier stages of its development lyric poetry had treated the subject of death primarily as a metaphor for separation. Hyperbolically depicting his feeling of loneliness and despair, the troubadour and his successors regularly equated the lady's rejection with death. The widespread disasters of the late Middle Ages, both naturally and humanly generated, and an attendant sense of doom did much to restore a literal significance to the theme.

In the light of these observations, it is surprising to find a relative lack of emphasis on mortality in the poetry of Charles d'Orléans. This absence of interest is even more remarkable given the poet's firsthand acquaintance with social and personal tragedy. References to death are comparatively few and mainly follow the formulaic patterns of the troubadours and trouvères. Reflections on mortality center less on the end of life than on the manner in which time is spent or wasted:

> Se j'ay mon temps mal despendu,
> Fait l'ay, par conseil de Follye;
> > (1:179)

> (If I have misspent my time,
> I have done so on the advice of Madness;)

It is imperative, therefore, that the present be kept free of the burdens that encumbered the past:

> Pour Dieu, laissons dormir Traveil;
> Ce mondes n'a gueres duree,

> Et Paine, tant qu'elle a sommeil,
> Souffrons que pregne resposee.
> > (1:180)

> (For God's sake, let's let Worry sleep;
> This world does not last long,
> And let's allow Torment,
> As long as she's sleepy, to rest.)

Traveil and Peine are only temporarily inactive and
will soon awake on their own. The folly of human nature is to provoke mental anguish where none need
exist. In begging that Worry and Torment be left in
peace the poet reminds us that much of our suffering is
self-inflicted.

Every meditation on mortality entails, of course,
some attention to the nature of time. On this point
Charles yields the word to aphoristic wisdom:

> Le temps passe comme le vent,
> Il n'est si beau jeu qui ne cesse,
> > (1:174)

> (Time passes like the wind,
> No game is so fine that it doesn't end,)

As a trite commentary on a brief love affair, the
adage, "Il n'est si beau jeu..." would be appropriately
used. Applied to life itself, the proverb discloses an
essential truth. Compressed into a single octosyllabic
utterance lies a recognition of one of the most mysterious and tragic elements of human existence. Perhaps we
should approach the verse not as a flippant degradation, the reduction of life to a mere game, but as an
extrapolation, an attempt to explain a natural phenomenon by analogy to a device of human invention.

Reading

In searching for figurative language to express his
thoughts, Charles often turned to daily occupations
which he found to be a rich source of metaphorical
imagery. Such prosaic activities as travel and oversee-
ing financial transactions are frequently exploited to

express a variety of more cerebral pursuits. One of the activities most successfully integrated into his poetry is the act of reading. Inclined by his nature and increasingly sedentary way of life, Charles devoted a large portion of his later years to poring over books on literary, scientific, and philosophical subjects. He did much of this reading in the study of Blois, a room we see transposed below into an allegorical context. The poet has just asked his heart if he has saved any token as a reminder of past service to Love:

> Aprés entrer je le veoye
> En ung comptouer qu'il avoit;
> La deça et dela queroit,
> En cherchant plusieurs vieulx cayers,
> Car le vray monstrer me vouloit,
> Mais qu'eust visité ses papiers.
>
> (1:152)

> (Afterwards I saw him enter
> A study that he had;
> And he searched here and there
> Looking for some old notebooks,
> For he wanted to show me the right one,
> But first he had to consult his papers.)

The heart's environment, as will be recalled, remains rather vague in the earlier ballads, usually just concrete enough to suggest confinement. Here the heart is shown entering a clearly defined chamber from which he will later emerge with the book he was seeking. At first glance, the image of the heart may seem to be the same with which we are acquainted from the exile poems. But in fact he, like the poet, has aged. Having retired from Love's service, he now shuffles about looking absent-mindedly for misplaced memories. In England Charles had let the heart act out one aspect of his personality. Now in a curious reversal he casts himself in the role of the heart. Who else if not the poet are we to see in the figure entering the study and rummaging among old notebooks and papers? And how can we dissociate the book of memories from the volume of verse Charles brought back from England?

Continuing to mix figurative images with realistic

detail taken from personal experience, the poet claims
in another ballad that his "reading ability" has become
impaired:

> Or, maintenant que deviens vieulx,
> Quant je lys ou livre de Joie,
> Les lunectes prens pour le mieulx,
>   (1:150)

> (Now that I am getting old,
> When I read out of the book of Joy,
> I put on my glasses, the better to see,)

The fact that Charles's eyesight was gradually
weakening at the time he wrote these verses is
secondary to the humor of the poet's complaint based on
the unexpected intrusion of personal experience into a
metaphorical statement.

Again taking the act of reading in a larger sense,
he claims he has lost the ability to decipher the
subtleties of worldly intrigue. He portrays himself as
a slow or naive schoolboy for whom everything must be
spelled out (in both senses):

> Escollier de Merencolie,
> A l'estude je suis venu,
> Lettres de mondaine clergie
> Espelant a tout ung festu.
> Et moult fort m'y treuve esperdu.
> Lire n'escripre ne sçay mye,
> Dez verges de Soussy batu,
> Es derreniers jours de ma vie.
>   (1:178)

> (A pupil of Melancholy,
> I have come to study,
> Spelling out with a straw*
> The letters of worldly education.
> And I find myself totally lost.
> Of reading or writing I know nothing,
> Beaten by the switches of Worry,
> In the last days of my life.) (1)

> *Used as an aid by schoolchildren.

Like Villon who regresses at the end of the Testament

to a "povre petit escollier" ("poor little schoolboy"),
Charles returns here to his distant past. While one
may choose to assign a literal meaning to the verse
"Lire n'escripre ne sçay mye" (the poet also experienced physical difficulty in writing during his later
years), a symbolic interpretation better fits the
spirit of the poem. What baffles the poet, if we are
to take him at his word, are the "letters of worldly
education," a system of signs that he is unable to
decode. Whether he is mocking himself or the complexity of his young friends' intrigues is not clear. In
either case we may be sure that, despite claims to the
contrary, the quick-witted duke was far from senile,
and hardly needed a straw to help him read the petty
schemes that were an integral part of any fifteenth-
century court.

If isolated from its context, the refrain would
appear a solemn or even gloomy reflection on the brevity of life. Any such pretensions, however, are undercut by the farcical nature of the preceding scene show-
ing the class dunce being whipped for not knowing his
lesson. A potentially painful subject, as we have seen
it happen before, is effectively disarmed by means of
irresistible humor. The messages of frustration and of
isolation from a younger generation are communicated,
but in such a manner as to elicit admiration instead of
pity.

The Inner Journey

Although Charles preferred to spend most of his time
comfortably installed at Blois, he did occasionally
venture out on short excursions. This travel was undertaken sometimes out of necessity (to attend a meeting
called by the king, or preside over a local festivity),
or sometimes simply as a means of breaking the monotony
of the daily routine. Where travel occurs as a well
developed motif, we find it in the later rather than
the earlier ballads. What is remarkable is the relative absence of physical motion in Charles's verse.
His is basically a quiescent poetry, impervious to
external commotion. The impression created throughout
the ballads is one of tranquil stability. The role
consistently favored by the poet is that of motionless
spectator.

In accordance with this static viewpoint, references

to travel are predictably limited to introspective
exploration. A trip down the Loire from Orléans to
Blois serves as the inspiration for one such internal
voyage. Sighting several river craft sailing under a
full wind, the poet characteristically transposes the
scene into allegorical terms. The heart, addressing
the poet and _Penser_ (Thought), explains his predica-
ment using nautical analogies in a passage exemplifying
the cohesiveness of sustained allegory in Charles's
later ballads:

> Mais je trueve le plus des mois
> L'eaue de Fortune si quoye,
> Quant ou bateau du Monde vois,
> Que, s'avirons d'Espoir n'avoye,
> Souvent en chemin demouroye,
>   (1:154)

> (But during most months I find
> The water of Fortune so calm
> When I travel in my boat of the World,
> That if I did not have oars of Hope
> I would often remain [stranded] in the
>   course,)

Four centuries later Rimbaud will take up the symbols
of the boat and the river in his "Bateau ivre": "Comme
je descendais des Fleuves impassibles..." ("As I was
going down impassive Rivers..."). Given impetus by the
success of the _Roman de la Rose_, allegory had come
into wide and often reckless use by the end of the medieval period. Poets who lacked the expertise required
to manipulate this technique effectively delighted in
carelessly stringing together one allegorical figure
after another. The resulting impression is often one
of disjointedness and incoherence. Charles's handling
of allegory, however, demonstrates a competence worthy
of Guillaume de Lorris, one of his earliest mentors.
In the verses quoted above, the allegorical representations are limited to four in number: Heart, the helms-
man; World, his boat; Hope, his oars; and Fortune, the
river. Each element of the allegory defines itself in
relation to the other elements. The separate images
are crafted not to stand alone, but to fit harmoniously
into the overall design. This ability to visualize a
larger pattern, along with consistent attention to de-

tail, form the essential ingredients of balanced and coherent allegory.

The poem returns in its conclusion to the river scene which initially inspired the poet's inner wandering:

> Les nefs dont cy devant parloye
> Montoient, et je descendoye
> Contre les vagues de Tourment;
>
> (The boats of which I was speaking
> Were going upstream, and I, going down,
> Against the waves of Worry;)

The vagues de Tourment provide a smooth and almost imperceptible transition from the exterior to the interior voyage. It is fitting that the poet's boat should be pictured floating passively with the current. Ironically it is his boat instead of those sailing upstream that encounters resistance. Here a minor defect appears in the allegorical fabric of the poem. The contradiction is not a matter of faulty nautical knowledge, for various natural phenomena could explain the waves moving against the current, but rather a lack of consistency in the imagery. The water element, which was previously equated with Fortune, or external circumstances, is now associated with Tourment, a state of mind. The flaw, admittedly, is a small one, and serves as a reminder of the complexity of the poet's difficult art.

An overland journey supplies the model for another extended allegory:

> En la forest de Longue Actente,
> Chevauchant par divers sentiers
> M'en voys, ceste annee presente,
> Ou voyage de Desiriers.
> Devant sont allez mes fourriers*
> Pour appareiller mon logeis
> En la cité de Destinee;
>
> (1:165)
>
> (In the forest of Long Waiting,
> Following various paths,
> I ride, this present year,
> On the journey of Desire.

My servants have gone ahead
To ready my quarters
In the city of Destiny;)

    *fourriers - servants responsible for
preparing the lodging.

Based on actual customs of the day, the poem contains a
wealth of concrete detail. Charles describes an expedition of over one hundred horses, mentions accompanying
officers, baggage, pack horses, and worries about quar-
tering the members of his entourage if sufficient lodging cannot be found in commercial establishments.   As
for himself, he will be spending the night in the
ostellerie de Pensee ("the inn of Thought").
    The introduction of such banalities as baggage and
pack horses into a poem dealing with destiny and fortune may strike the modern reader as incongruous if not
ludicrous.   To infer, however, that this poem and ones
like it were not meant by their author to be taken seriously would be a mistake.   Charles in his later years
continued to be fascinated by allegorization as a method of exploring inner space.   One of his most important
achievements lies in his willingness to tap new sources
of imagery while remaining loyal to traditional forms
and techniques.

Commercial Transactions

    Besides sickness and travel, another aspect of daily
life that Charles successfully integrates into his
later ballads is commerce. Commercial language provides a novel and effective medium for describing a
variety of personal attitudes, especially when these
are tinged with cynicism. Protesting against Youth's
capricious decision to hand him over to Old Age,
Charles in the earlier phase of his poetry might typically have branded the act as one of treason. Now, his
former idealistic fervor having cooled a bit, he
chooses to present the transfer as part of a simple
financial transaction:

        Pourquoy m'as tu vendu, Jennesse,
        A grant marchié, comme pour riens...?
                                    (1:183)

(Why have you sold me, Youth,
At a cheap price, for almost nothing...?)

The most frequent application of commercial language
occurs, as one might expect, in connection with love.
Transplanted into the sphere of financial activity, mat-
ters of the heart are reduced to obeying the predict-
able influence of economic law. Once understood in
these tangible terms, love is quickly stripped of its
mystery:

> Ce que l'ueil despend en plaisir,
> Le cuer l'achete chierement,
> (1:173)

> (What the eye spends on pleasure,
> The heart purchases dearly,)

Continuing the analogy, the poet presents Reason as a
sort of financial officer or auditor who demands a complete account of all the expenditures covered by
"Love's wealth."

In another ballad the motifs of travel and commerce
are combined to represent the undertaking of a personal
enterprise whose nature is never disclosed:

> Dieu vueille sauver ma galee
> Qu'ay chargee de marchandise
> (1:169)

> (May God protect my merchant vessel
> Which I have loaded with goods)

He asks that the ship be protected from pirates, winds,
and high seas, and states that he has supplied a guide-
book to facilitate navigation in foreign waters. Continuing the use of commercial language, the poet describes the ship's mission:

> Pour acquitter joye empruntee
> L'envoye, sans espargner mise;

> (To pay off borrowed joy
> I send it, without sparing
> expense;)

No further clues are given to the symbolism of the merchant ship.

This mysterious vessel raises a problematic aspect of Charles's poetry that we have already encountered in the ballad on the mirror. Certain images, although obviously invested with a personal meaning, remain impenetrable to any amount of probing. It is this opaque quality that occasionally makes his work appear inaccessible to the modern reader. In all likelihood the members of Charles's circle who were closest to him—his wife, his physician, such favorite acquaintances as Benoist Damien and Gilles des Ormes—were privy to personal information, since lost, that gave them a special insight into the duke's poetry. This does not mean that his work must be approached by the twentieth-century reader as a hermetically sealed world into which our entrance is forbidden. From the standpoint of literary criticism the question of factual foundation cannot be regarded as a primary consideration. More important are the poetic patterns created by images whose true private significance must remain the poet's secret.

Vocabulary

By now it should be evident that certain appreciable differences separate the earlier and later groups of ballads. The first cycle, unified by themes stemming from love and separation, relies heavily on abstractions, words such as <u>amour</u>, <u>espoir</u>, <u>penser</u>, <u>loyauté</u> appearing frequently. Verbs relate mainly to communication, verbal and written, as well as to memory, thought, emotion, and volition. The second cycle of ballads, while retaining familiar lexical patterns, also shows some new and imaginative configurations. More rigorous and energetic verb usage gives the verse increased vigor. Abstract vocabulary is now frequently punctuated by a variety of concrete terms, as allegorical representation is extended and modeled more closely on mundane activities. This introduction of the commonplace into a literary discourse whose suppleness rests on a lack of verbal precision creates new possibilities for graphic expression. Pillaging semantic fields not normally associated with lyric verse, Charles enriches his poetic vocabulary as well as his repertoire of images.

By way of summary and synthesis, the following abbreviated list offers a sampling of the areas from which "trivial" language is most frequently drawn:

Work / Professions:
    astronomians (astrologer)   officier
    gaiges (wages)   physiciens
            (physician)

Commerce / Finance:
    acheter (purchase)   espargne (savings)
    debte   grant marchié
            (cheap)

Travel:
    bagaiges   ostellerie (inn)
    chevaucher (ride on   sommier (pack horse)
      horseback)

Legal Procedure:
    advocat (lawyer)   plaidier (plead a
    huissier (bailiff)   case)
            seeau (seal)

Medicine:
    cirugie (surgery)   enfler (to swell)
    enrumé (congested)   frissonner (to
            shake)

Even with its gradual expansion dating from Charles's return to France, the lexical breadth of the ballads remains relatively narrow. To a total of 1,790 different words in all the ballads, one need only compare the corpus of Villon (2,950 words) or Baudelaire (over 4,000 in Les Fleurs du Mal) to appreciate the modest dimensions of Charles's poetic vocabulary. Despite his wanderings into regions of language generally regarded as foreign to the lyric tradition, Charles, like the seventeenth-century writers of tragedy, felt most at ease working with a classically austere vocabulary.

Conclusion

In spite of certain dissimilarities, the ballads of the first and second cycle hold much in common. The

subject of love, although now viewed through a different optic, continues to draw substantial attention.
The use of allegory continues to develop along the
imaginative lines already sketched in the earlier ballads. New thematic material has been introduced, old
preoccupations are treated in novel ways, but the focus
remains basically unchanged. Throughout the ballads
the poet directs our attention not to the world without
but to the world within. Now and then a scene from
fifteenth-century England or France will briefly appear, but only as a pretext for entry into the poet's
mind. The boats on the river are duly noted, but the
vessel sailing through the poetic imagination proves
much more interesting.

Chapter Ten
The Rondeaux

The ballad furnished Charles considerable latitude for developing his line of thought in either simple or elaborated form, and through systematic usage of the genre he learned to manipulate it in a competent and often sophisticated fashion. It is for his rondeaux, however, that he is best known. Perhaps it was the highly musical quality of the genre that most appealed to him. He may have been attracted primarily by its compact form, which places a premium on verbal concision, or by the exigencies of its metrical structure. Whatever facet of the rondeau most endeared it to him, the form captured and held his fancy during the years following his release from England. Under his hand the rondeau was polished, if any poetic genre can be said to have been, to perfection. No historical anthology of French poetry would be complete without at least one rondeau by Charles d'Orléans.

The art of the rondeau is one that demands a sensitive ear and a delicate touch. Fluidity of movement is essential, yet metric constraints need not vitiate the content of the poem. The challenge is to develop a thought, mood, or scene within the allotted spatial limitations and without breaking the musical rhythm which is essential to the form. The creation of images within rigorously defined spatial boundaries brings to mind the art of the manuscript illuminator. Indeed the medieval mind seemed to have delighted in surrounding the creative act with the most rigid restrictions. A more enlightening comparison, taken again from the graphic arts, is provided by the example of the black and white drawings of Henri Matisse (1). With remarkably few but boldly drawn lines, the artist creates images of striking beauty and simplicity which, some would say, represent better than his paintings the quintessence of his art. Like the drawings of Matisse, the rondeaux of Charles d'Orléans contain only the sparsest detail, and yet consistently produce an impression of rich harmony. Charles's little poems are in fact sketches which reduce their subject to its most basic lines, and represent it with minimal elaboration.

Charles used the rondeau, unlike the ballad, as a vehicle for conveying a wide variety of themes. While the ballad is almost always inwardly focused, the scope of the rondeau includes vistas from outside as well as inside the poet's mind. Commentaries on society, satirical remarks directed at a certain individual or type of individual, references to specific circumstances--a trip, the reception of a visitor--scenes taken from nature, all abound in these poems. To be sure, some themes and techniques of the ballads are duplicated, but sufficient differences exist to warrant a separate examination of this particular genre.

History and Form

The rondeau's ancestry may be traced to the <u>rondet de carole</u>, a lively paced dance song. The <u>etymo-logical</u> root <u>rond</u> ("round") comes from the circular form of the song which closes with a repetition of its opening verses. Adam de la Halle and Guillaume de Machaut both composed rondeaux as a musical genre. The form appears as a poetic genre in Deschamps's <u>Art de dictier</u> where it bears the label of <u>rondel</u> (2). Clément Marot and Vincent Voiture wrote rondeaux in the sixteenth and seventeenth centuries respectively, and Voltaire and Musset were among later writers who tried their hand at this form, by then considered charmingly antiquated.

Although the rondeau form may vary considerably from one poet to another, a few general observations may be made by way of a loose definition. The poem consists of three stanzas, each of which may contain from two to six verses. Versification is based on two rhymes, but no fixed rhyme pattern is prescribed. Part of the opening stanza is repeated at the end of the second and third stanzas, and the last stanza tends to be slightly longer than the first two.

One of the reasons why the rondeau cannot be neatly defined is the problem posed by a certain scribal convention called the <u>rentrement</u> ("re-entry"). As a means of economizing space the poem's refrain was routinely curtailed to its first few words followed by the abbreviation <u>etc</u>. This raises the question of how

much of the opening stanza the poet intends to repeat--
just the first verse, the first two verses, perhaps the
whole stanza? Champion's interpretations vary. Often
he includes two verses of the refrain at the end of the
second stanza, and only the first verse at the end of
the third. Or the pattern may be reversed. Sometimes
he limits the refrain to one verse in the third as well
as in the second stanza. Or the first two verses of
the opening stanza may appear in both of the others.
Champion, exercising his prerogative as an editor,
relies on a subjective reading of each poem in determin-
ing how to distribute the verses of the refrain. It
should be remembered that the bracketed portions of the
text are to be read as editorial interpretation, as in
the case of punctuation and capitalization. While discreet editorial intervention is useful and often enlightening in the transposition of the text from manuscript to printed page, it may also be misleading. The
etc. is meant to throw the eye back to the first stanza. The quantity of verses actually reread will vary
from one reader to another (3).

In Charles's rondeaux the most common arrangement of
verses into stanzas follows the model: 4 / 3 / 5, if
the rentrement is counted as a single verse. The typical rhyme scheme is ABba / abR / abbaR, the capital-
ized letters representing the refrain. Octosyllabic
meter is the overwhelming preference, although verses
of ten or six syllables are occasionally used.

In his exploration of various existing verse forms,
Charles d'Orléans, to our knowledge at least, never
tried his hand at the sonnet. Given his admiration for
Italian culture and his love of poetry, it seems highly
unlikely that he was never exposed to the sonnets of
Petrarch. Although both the rondeau and the sonnet are
tightly compact poetic forms, they are separated by
certain fundamental differences which may explain
Charles's attraction for one and indifference to the
other. The Italian genre progresses in linear fashion
to a culmination accentuated by the shortening of the
closing stanzas. The French form, on the other hand,
moves in a circular direction and ends with an invita-
tion to a second reading. With its dance-song tempo
the rondeau would have been poorly suited to bear the
weight of scholarly references with which the Renaissance poets would load the sonnet.

Personal Circumstance

As his vast output of rondeaux suggests, Charles did
not have to search far for inspiration. He found virtually any subject suitable for these little poems. Many
seem to have been composed almost on the spur of the
moment, so obvious is the link between the poem and its
immediate stimulus. In one such piece he warmly thanks
his dear friend René d'Anjou for a gift recently received. In another he bids farewell to a house guest,
Charles de Nevers, requesting that his visitor leave
his heart behind in payment for the fine hospitality.
He speaks of a treaty conference attended in Tours, of
going to Orléans to watch a tournament, complains of
travel undertaken in unfavorable weather. Finding himself bored with an excursion into the countryside of
Touraine, he expresses, with an appropriately rural
image, his longing to return home:

> Je ne hanis pour autre avaine
> Que de m'en retourner a Blois;
> Trouvé me suis, pour une fois,
> Assez longuement en Touraine.
> (2:415)

> (I whinney after no other oats
> But to return to Blois;
> I find I have stayed, for once,
> Long enough in Touraine.)

In verses reminiscent of Colin Muset, the thriteenth-
century trouvère who sang of food, drink, and travel,
Charles goes on to confess that his palate has been
sated by ample quantities of local fish and wine, and
makes it clear that provincial existence is no match
for court life.

These particular poems, each specifically linked to
a minor event or circumstance in the poet's life, clearly do not constitute one of Charles's greatest literary
achievements. Yet they are among his most interesting
pieces. Through them we are given a glimpse of how he
spent his time when not reading or writing. These rondeaux make up a sort of souvenir scrapbook from which
we may attempt to reconstruct portions of the poet's
daily life.

Equally important, the use of everyday scenes as

subjects for his rondeaux tells us something about
Charles's evolving concept of poetry. The ballads and
songs written in England chronicle stages of his spiritual life. Now he seeks to record worldly events as
well. The expansion of language displayed in the later
ballads is paralleled by an expansion of subject matter
in the rondeaux.

Nature

Among the most vivid scenes of Charles's rondeaux
are those taken from the poet's natural environment.
Above all he is fascinated by the seasonal cycle and
its effects upon the psyche. Nature, of course, is one
of the oldest topoi in lyric poetry. The troubadours
and trouvères were constantly singing of spring as a
time of renewed joy and hope. But the motifs traditionally associated with seasonal change serve merely as a
pretext for the poet to expose his emotional state, a
state which either harmonizes or contrasts with his surroundings. Nature itself does little more than set the
mood of the poem, and thus plays a peripheral role.
Unlike his predecessors, Charles is willing to utilize
natural scenery as a focus for his poetry. In so doing
he generally avoids recourse to the standard formulaic
descriptions, preferring to draw his imagery from the
resources of his own imagination.

Given the dimensional restrictions imposed by the
rondeau, Charles's descriptions are of necessity terse
and highly selective. Deprived of the luxury of space,
a limitation unknown to the Romantic poets who could
indulge in lengthy eulogies of nature, he was forced to
economize his language to an extreme. This self-disci-
pline produced verse of exceptional clarity and suc-
cinctness. Rather than waste precious ink on flat
straightforward description, Charles preferred to
enrich his poetry with metaphorical imagery. His favorite technique was personification, a device he had come
to master in the ballads. Previously it had been the
intangibles--emotions, memory, destiny--that were portrayed as persons. Now the visible traces of time's
passage also take on human form:

> Les fourriers d'Esté sont venus
> Pour appareillier son logis,
> Et ont fait tendre ses tappis,

De fleurs et verdure tissus.
(2:307)

(The servants of Summer have come
To prepare his lodging,
And have spread out his rugs
Woven of flowers and greenery.)

The image of the rug woven of flowers and grass is a
particularly evocative one, relying on the reader's
imagination for its completion. One may easily visualize, for instance, a variety of vivid colors set
against a deep green background. The rug analogy also
suggests a unity of artistic design in the pattern of
the colors, and gives the scene a tactile appeal by
evoking a sense of luxuriant texture. By reducing a
vast landscape into a single logis, or dwelling, the
poet interiorizes an exterior space, the reverse of the
process frequently used in the ballads. The logis
also accentuates the transitory quality of the season
which, we are reminded, is only passing through.

By far the most famous of Charles's rondeaux, the
best known of all his poems, in fact, is the one in
which he compares the arrival of spring to a change of
garments:

Le temps a laissié son manteau
De vent, de froidure et de pluye,
Et s'est vestu de brouderie
De soleil luysant, cler et beau.[4]
(2:307)

(Time has shed its cloak
Of wind, cold, and rain,
And dressed in embroidery
Of shining, clear, and lovely sun.)

The equivocal use of temps permits us to read it
either as "the weather" or as "time." Either translation may be justified, but the latter provides a more
interesting reading. Taken in this sense, temps does
not stand for climatic conditions, but rather the element that remains steadfast and unchanging throughout
seasonal variations.

The poem's popularity may be explained not only by
its pleasing interior rhyme and captivating rhythm, but

also by the richness of its imagery. Working again
with textures, the poet contrasts the coarse outer garment of winter with the softer, lighter material of
spring. The transformation of sunlight into a delicate
fabric evokes a certain sensual quality, the touch of
light on skin. There is at the same time a visual
dimension to the image, the gold threads embroidered
into the garment eliciting a play of light and shadow.

Extending the metaphor of clothing, the poet describes the glittering effect of sun on flowing water:

> Riviere, fontaine et ruisseau
> Portent, en livree jolie,
> Gouttes d'argent d'orfaverie,
> (2:308)

> (River, brook, and stream
> Wear, as a pretty livery,
> Drops of wrought silver,)

The natural is again translated into the artificial.
Nature is seen not as a blindly moving force, but as a
consummate craftsman laboring purposefully and method-
ically to create designs of exquisite beauty and refinement.

While Charles uses personification as a means of describing nature, he also borrows examples from nature to
elucidate certain human behavior. He compares his love
for his lady to the fatal attaction of the moth to the
candle. In a moment of frustrated expectation he becomes a falcon confined to a cage while molting his
feathers and waiting to fly. In another poem he likens
the end of a period of dejection to the passing of a
violent storm:

> Quant Pleur ne pleut, Souspir ne vent,
> Et que cessee est la tourmente
> De Dueil...
> (2:451)

> (When Weeping does not rain, nor Sigh blow,
> And the storm of Grief has ceased,...)

Viewing his emotional turmoil as a natural phenomenon,
the poet reassures himself that it cannot last long.
In the rondeaux, that most cyclical of all poetic

forms, Charles shows a definite interest in cycles, whether of season or of the heart. Rather than stress the destructive phase of the process, as do many of his literary contemporaries, he frequently reminds us of its regenerative powers.

But the most important lesson drawn from nature is one of humility. Man's helplessness in the face of elemental forces serves as a reminder of his lack of control over his own destiny. To his readers Charles poses the question:

> Les en voulez vous garder
> Ces rivieres de courir
> Et grues prendre et tenir
> Quant hault les veez voler?
>   (2:372)

> (Do you want to keep
> These rivers from flowing,
> And catch and hold cranes
> When you see them flying high?)

"Why waste time trying to accomplish the impossible?" the poet asks. From rivers and cranes he moves to human nature and the subject of fate. Let time pass, we are admonished by a man speaking from personal experience, as Fortune wills it to pass.

Observations on Society

When not directed toward his natural surroundings, Charles's keen eye was frequently trained on the human element of his environment. Having become well acquainted with the aristocratic society of Touraine, Burgundy, Italy, and England, Charles was qualified to make generalizations valid beyond the confines of his native province. In an age rife with political intrigue he had witnessed countless acts of self-interest cloaked under every conceivable disguise. This duplicity in political dealings engendered a public attitude of mistrust which inevitably pervaded the whole of society, providing the poet with a rich source of material for his caustic observations.

Of particular interest to Charles was the relationship between society and the individual. The two, he notices, are habitually pitted against each other. So-

ciety is constantly seeking the individual's weakness,
always ready to exploit whatever it can find. The individual, in order to minimize his vulnerability, is
left with no choice but to conceal his true feelings:

> Plus penser que dire
> Me couvient souvent
> ....
> Faignant de sousrire
> Quant suis tresdolent,
> (2:315)

> (It often behooves me
> To think more than I say
> ....
> Pretending to smile
> When I am very sad,)

A feigned cough serves to cover a heartfelt sigh.
These ploys and others like them keep the poet's feelings from being discovered, insuring him a privé mar-
tire, a private martyrdom.

Aware of the potential dangers of unbridled speech,
Charles counsels us to speak with restraint, monitor
our words carefully, and hold back at least a portion
of our thoughts:

> Quelque chose derriere
> Couvient toujours garder,
> On ne peut pas monstrer
> Sa voulenté entiere.
> (2:328)

> (It is best to keep
> Something back,
> One cannot show
> His full intention.)

One can, obviously, reveal his full intention if he
wishes, but to do so would invite trouble. La
Rochefoucauld makes a similar observation: "La con-
stance des sages n'est que l'art de renfermer leur agitation dans le coeur" (5). ("The strength of wise men
is no more than the art of closing up their agitation
in their heart.") La Rochefoucauld's Maximes, incidentally, form an interesting parallel to Charles's

remarks on society. Both writers, viewing their societies from the same aristocratic perspective, stress the
duplicitous nature of the human character, its tendency
to allow petty motives to masquerade as noble virtues.
Both delight in unmasking hypocrisy in all its forms,
always measuring the gap between reality and appearance.

The influence of society upon the individual, as
Charles sees it, is a corruptive one. Rather than take
the chance of provoking difficulty by telling the
truth, he finds lying a more effective recourse:

> Mieulx vault mentir pour paix avoir
> Qu'estre batu pour dire voir;
>
> (2:375)

> (It is better to lie to have peace
> Than to be beaten for telling the truth;)

To interpret these verses as an admonition to practice
immoral behavior when expedient would be to misread the
poet's intent. His thoughts on lying should be taken
as seriously as his fear of being beaten for telling
the truth. His point is simply that honesty has no
part in the game played by society. Therefore, to suc-
ceed in the game one would be well advised to play by
the rules.

The only type of person immune to societal influence
is one who has given up his dignity:

> Qui a toutes ses hontes beues,
> Il ne lui chault que l'en lui die,
> Il laisse passer mocquerie
> Devant ses yeulx, comme les nues.
>
> (2:405)

> (He who has drunk all his shames
> Does not care what people may say to him,
> He lets mockery pass
> Before his eyes, like clouds.)

The phrase "toutes...hontes beues" occurs in the second
verse of Villon's Testament, and it has been suggested that it was with the young poet in mind that Charles
wrote these lines. Whether or not Villon is actually
the subject of the poem, it is clear that Charles ex-

periences a certain sympathy and even a touch of admiration for the type of man who by sacrificing his self-
esteem manages to remain indifferent to social abuse.

Those who are not strong-willed or degraded enough
to resist public opinion run the risk of falling into
hypocrisy. Hypocrites, especially those who are women,
are one of Charles's favorite subjects of attack. In
one poem he warns us not to trust appearances, using as
a point of departure the proverb, "L'abit le moyne ne
fait pas" ("the habit does not make the monk"). In
another he derides those people who believe they are
terribly clever, but who fail to recognize when they
are making fools out of themselves. Unlike La
Rochefoucauld, whose acerbic wit is often tinged with a
touch of self-righteousness, Charles's remarks are made
more in the spirit of detached observation than moralistic commentary. Human behavior may occasionally provoke a gentle reproach, but it is always a reproach
accompanied by an indulgent smile.

Satire

Charles in his later years, as we have seen, depended for entertainment on younger high-spirited companions whose company he cherished. Their adventures,
ambitions, aspirations, and failures supplied him with
constant amusement. As a detached observer he could
enjoy the comical aspects of their exaggerated pride,
and he delighted in mocking their serious pretensions.
Sometimes he singles out a companion by name, teasing
him about an embarrassing incident which is by now a
matter of public knowledge. More often it is the whole
group of individuals that is targeted. The favorite
line of attack is the one to which his young friends
are the most vulnerable, the theme of love. With
feigned concern for

> Les malades cueurs amoureux
> Qui ont perdu leurs appetis,
> (2:358)

> (The lovesick hearts
> Who have lost their appetites,)

the poet prescribes an herbal remedy composed, among
other ingredients, of the flower of Memory and the root

of Jealousy, a good dose of which is to be taken just
before bedtime. Questioning the fidelity of these love-
lorn young men and the sincerity of their commitment,
he offers his mock admiration:

> Ces beaux mignons a vendre et a revendre,
> Regardez les, sont ilz pas a louer?
>
> (2:491)

> (These charming beaus for sale and resale,
> Look at them, aren't they to be praised?)

A play on louer allows the second verse to also read,
"....aren't they for rent?" If the duke lent a sympa-
thetic ear to the tribulations of his infatuated companions, no evidence is to be found in his poetry.

Perhaps the most interesting aspect of Charles's
satirical verse is what it reveals about his state of
mind. He watches the follies and petty conflicts of
human nature with the same detachment he displays when
observing the passage of the seasons. He continually
manifests an awareness of the movement of time, whether
made visible through nature or humanity. This sense of
temporal motion is accentuated by the revolving motion
of the rondeau itself. Life begins, dies, and is re-
born according to the seasons. Passion is followed by
peace of mind, which is succeeded by a new passion.
All things move in cycles. Grounded on this wisdom,
the poet's perspective enables him to view the minor
upheavals of human existence within a larger context
than that available to those entrapped in these events.
Conceived as essentially futile, man's ambitions may be
interpreted either as basically tragic or comic.
Charles's rondeaux are anything but tragic.

Perhaps the best indication of his attitude is to be
found in a rondeau inspired by the sight of some enthusiastic young men departing for a bird hunt during the
winter. They are elegantly dressed in the latest fashion, obviously well pleased with their appearance but
poorly protected by their scanty attire against the rigors of winter weather.

> Laissez aler ces gorgias,
> Chascun yver, a la pippee;
> Vous verrez comme la gelee

> Reverdira leurs estomas.
> (2:295)
>
> (Let these dandies go,
> Each winter, on the bird hunt;
> You will see how the frost
> Will turn their stomachs green.)

The hunters, caught up in the excitement of the moment, remain oblivious to the possible consequences of their vanity. The poet, amused by the thought of the coming contest between pride and elemental necessity, looks forward to seeing how elegant the party will look at the end of the hunt. Still, he recognizes that, perennial as the winter itself, the scene will be enacted again and again.

Self-Portraits

The ballads and songs present a whole gamut of feelings: longing, fear, grief, joy, and hope. We therefore become intimately acquainted with the poet's emotional life, while remaining relatively ignorant of his thoughts. How does he perceive his past and present life? How does he see himself in relation to others? What sort of self-image does he have? What philosophy, if any, has he adopted as a practical guide by which to live? These questions are never directly answered in the rondeaux, but at least a few hints are scattered here and there. One of the most important signs of Charles's maturity as a poet is his ability to step back a bit and describe himself from a certain distance. In so doing, he shows no more clemency for himself than for those who are the targets of his satire.

Concerning his physical state, the poet is terse and blunt:

> Je deviens viel, sourt et lourt
> (2:540)
>
> (I'm getting old, deaf, and heavy).

We are also informed that his hair is white, that he can no longer draw back a bowstring without hurting his arm, and that, like a lazy cat, he does not wake up

easily. Whether through absent-mindedness or indifference, his attention often wanders:

> Ce qui m'entre par une oreille,
> Par l'autre sault, com est venu,
>   (2:327)

> (What enters through one ear,
> Goes out through the other, as it came,)

In the ballads Charles, as we have seen, typically
chooses to portray his state of mind through allegorical imagery. In the rondeaux he often speaks of himself in more direct terms, creating a less fragmented
and more readily apprehensible personality. He nostal-
gically recalls his youth and recognizes the distance
separating him from it. A lover's sigh triggers the
memory of similar "tricks" used in his younger days.
In a moment of moodiness he admits with a disarming
frankness characteristic of his later poetry:

> Le monde est ennuyé de moy,
> Et moy pareillement de lui;
>   (2:397)

> (The world is bored with me,
> And I also with it;)

With a hyperbolic note of tragedy, which it is difficult to take with complete seriousness, he asks rhetori-
cally who would be willing to exchange places with him,
claiming that no worse lot could be found anywhere.
But periods of sullenness are balanced by periods of
happiness. Fortunately there exists an infallible anti-
dote for the poet's boredom:

> Mais s'entour moy pluseurs je voy,
> Et qu'on rit, parle, chante ou crye,
> Je chasse hors Merencolye
>   (2:520)

> (But if I see several people around me,
> Laughing, talking, singing, or yelling,
> I chase away Melancholy)

The comment that reveals the most about the poet's

philosophical viewpoint is, again, prompted by a reference to hunting:

> Il ne me chault ne de chien ne d'oyseau;
> Quant tout est fait, il fault passer sa vie
> Le plus aise qu'on peut, en chiere lie.
>   (2:490)

> (I care nothing for dogs or birds;
> When all is done, life should be spent
> As comfortably as possible, in great ease.)

The poem is one of Charles's gayest pieces, celebrating
the joys of good living and cheerful company. The
verses are even more revealing if we take the "dogs and
birds" in a larger sense. The hunt, that honored and
almost sacred privilege of the nobility, is at once a
quest for adventure, a test of prowess, and a primal
rite symbolizing the superiority of the hunter over the
hunted. While never having been an avid sportsman,
Charles had tasted his share of ambition and failure,
and when he finally retired to Blois, he clearly did so
with the intention of renouncing the "hunt." Some may
read these verses as evidence of unabashed hedonism,
but Charles's outlook resists such convenient labeling.
Moreover, to call his attitude hedonistic would imply
an excessive indulgence in pleasure, and the poet's
life, to judge at least from all we know of it, was a
model of moderation.

Open and Shut Doors

In the early cycle of ballads Charles used structures of confinement, particularly of the heart, to
express his sense of isolation and loneliness. The
enclosure of the heart obviously parallels the hostage's loss of freedom. In the rondeaux we again encounter images based on the containment of the heart or
self, but in a new context. For now that the poet can
move about at will, the circumstances of his physical
existence can no longer be identified with references
to spatial containment. Instead it is a purely psychological facet of his existence that he means to represent, the key to which lies in the image of the door.
Doors, of course, have two basic functions, to allow
and to prevent entry. Charles, consistently finding

himself on the inside rather than the outside of the
enclosure, uses the object primarily as a means of keeping out uninvited visitors. These unwelcome callers
fall either into the category of negative emotions--Mel-
ancholy, Worry, and the others--or the senses, especially those of sight and hearing. To protect his serenity
from the threat of these pernicious influences, he re-
treats to an inner sanctum where he is guaranteed safety from unwanted intrusion.

The assault of anxiety upon the psyche is usually
represented in the early ballads by military imagery.
The poet barricades himself within the fortress of his
thought and prepares to defend himself against the
attack of his persistent enemies. The rondeaux, by
contrast, portray the same assault in less dynamic
terms. The confrontation is more often verbal than
violent. The poet's former adversaries have by now
become familiar acquaintances. Still, they are acquaintances whose company he seeks to avoid. The
importune arrival of Melancholy generally elicits a
nominally polite but firm rebuff. In a typical response Charles reminds her that her presence has not
been requested, and flatly directs her to return to
where she came from, and to take her companion with
her:

> Soussi avecques vous menez,
> Mon huys ne vous ouvreray mie:
> (2:523)

> (Take Worry with you,
> I will not open my door to you at all:)

The change of metaphorical representation reveals an
interesting shift of psychological perspective. Viewed
as assailants, Melancholy, Worry, Sadness, and the
other members of their host constituted a force beyond
the poet's control. His only choice was to seek refuge
and endure their brief or prolonged attack. Now, having realized that these undesirable elements, being
creations of his own mind, are only as potent as he
permits them to be, he uses the door to symbolize the
power of his volition to shut out subversive influences.

Sometimes it is the poet we find behind the door,
sometimes it is his heart or his thought:

> Ne hurtez plus a l'uis de ma Pensee,
> Soing et Soussi, sans tant vous traveiller,
> Car elle dort et ne veult s'esveiller,
> (2:462)

(Don't knock on the door of my Thought,
Care and Worry, causing yourselves so much
  trouble,
For she is sleeping and does not wish to
  wake)

Separating a part of himself from his thought, the poet transcends the potential mental conflict and observes the scene from a comfortable distance. This is a type of dissociation we have already seen effected between the "I" and the heart. In that case, however, the operative principle was understood to be the identification of the "I" with reason. In this instance the opposition is evidently one of a different nature, for the voice of the poem claims detachment not from emotion but from thought itself. If not reason, then, the source of the voice must be some mode of perception unallied with the analytical faculties of the mind. It is from this disengaged position that he watches Worry and Care vainly attempting to enter the realm of his thought.

  Intrusion of the senses, like that of the emotions, threatens to destroy the equilibrium on which the poet's tranquillity depends:

> Par les portes dez yeulx et dez oreilles,
> Que chascun doit bien sagement garder,
> Plaisir Mondain va et vient, sans cesser,
> Et raporte de diverses merveilles.
> (2:332)

(Through the doors of the eyes and the ears,
Which each person must wisely guard,
Worldly Pleasure comes and goes, without cease,
And reports various marvels.)

While the door may be closed in the face of Melancholy and Worry, messages from the senses cannot be so easily blocked. They can, however, be censored. The senses are dangerous for two reasons. First, they might tempt the heart to trade its cherished peace and seclusion

for the excitement of worldly pursuits. Second, they
are deceiving and therefore not to be trusted.

The nature of the enticement offered by the senses
is not left entirely vague. A number of explicit hints
suggest that the culprit is feminine beauty. The eyes,
for example, are always being scolded for disturbing
the heart's much-needed rest by bringing it images of
loveliness. The description of the eyes as windows of
the heart, an old courtly conceit, also occurs in the
rondeaux. If we are to believe his poetry, the duke
was never completely beyond the reach of temptation.

Religious Imagery

Although not a major theme in the rondeaux, religion
does serve as a favorite source of metaphorical description. By the fifteenth century religious language
already had a long history of association with the
French lyric. It was originally used to express the
poet's veneration for his lady, and the parallel between early hymns to the Virgin and certain chansons
d'amour has led some scholars to posit one as the origin of the other, although they cannot agree on which
one is the imitation. Charles, on the other hand,
employs religious imagery primarily to describe his
mental state. It is especially in the areas of theology and monastic life that he seeks examples applicable
to his existence. These analogies, generally carrying
a slightly ascetic flavor, often underscore the poet's
renunciation--or, to be more accurate, his alleged re-
nunciation--of worldly pleasures.

Life at the end of the medieval period, it must be
remembered, was saturated with religion. Huizinga
paints an eloquent picture of an existence based on the
rhythm of holy days and masses, accompanied by the
almost continual ringing of bells. Charles's day, like
that of any other nobleman, was punctuated and given
order by a variety of religious ceremonies. It seems
only natural then that this important facet of his
life, like so many others, eventually penetrated his
poetry. To be sure, he had already experimented with
religious imagery in the early ballads, but only on a
very limited scale. In the rondeaux we see the technique used more extensively, more imaginatively, and
with greater breadth of application.

Comparing the lot of unsuccessful lovers to that of

damned souls, Charles pleads with those of the female
sex to treat their victims with more charity:

> Dedens l'abisme de douleur,
> Sont tourmentees povres ames
> Des amans;
>
> (2:370)

> (Within the abyss of sorrow,
> Are tormented the poor souls
> Of lovers;)

Blending courtly tradition here with popular theology,
he creates a more graphic portrayal of the lover's suffering than the vague descriptions conventionally offered by previous and contemporary poets. His own soul
is pictured not in Hell but in Purgatory:

> Une povre ame tourmentee
> Ou Purgatoire de Soussy,
> Est en mon corps...
>
> (2:493)

> (A poor soul tormented
> In the Purgatory of Worry
> Is in my body...)

It is indeed rare that the poet speaks of his own soul,
and the word _ame_, used without the flippancy of the
previously cited reference to lovers' souls, sets a
more somber tone than that usually found in the rondeaux. The manner by which the soul is identified
reveals something of its place in Charles's poetry.
Although the possessive adjective is applied to the
body (_mon corps_) and later in the poem to the heart
(_mon cueur_), _ame_ is impersonally introduced by the
indefinite article _une_. Unlike the heart, the soul,
foreign to the poetic world, remains a stranger.

Reworking an image already used in an early ballad,
Charles portrays his heart as a religious hermit with-
drawing to the refuge of his hermitage. _Plaisant
Regard_ ("Pleasing Look") becomes an almoner, a profession traditionally carried out under the auspices
of the Church. His present life is the Lenten fasting, his youth, the period of feasting preceding Lent.
In another poem he compares the process of aging

to the changing of monastic order:

> J'ay gardé, ou temps de jeunesse,
> L'observance des amoureux.
> Or m'en a bouté hors Viellesse,
> Et mis en l'ordre douleureux.
>
> (2:354)

> (I kept, in the time of my youth,
> The rule of those in love.
> Now Old Age has expelled me,
> And put me in the sorrowful order.)

In the same rondeau he refers to himself as a "monk of Melancholy."

The one seemingly serious allusion to the poet's soul should not mislead us into thinking that all other religious references are necessarily to be taken in the same spirit. Granted, if found in the context of his earlier poetry, mention of monastic orders, fasting, and hermits could be interpreted as grim reminders of the psychological deprivation inflicted upon the hostage of war. But mixed as they are with poems of bantering and sarcastic tone, these religion-based images lend themselves to more than one interpretation, and it is difficult to say with certainty how seriously they are meant to be read. In spite of the sober connotations attached to certain words normally reserved for a sacred context, these same terms when appearing in Charles's rondeaux often seem to express more whimsy and wit than solemnity of thought. If so, the intention is clearly not to degrade the sanctity of religious institutions, but rather to appropriate yet another class of language for the purpose of irony.

Games, Tournaments, and Hunts

Conflict, both interpersonal and intrapersonal, frequently appears in the rondeaux under the guise of a sport or contest. The choice depends on the aspect of the conflict to be stressed. Board games imply a match of wits, and tournaments, a match of volition, while the hunt suggests a test of both. By circumscribing the conflict with clearly defined boundaries, and presenting it as governed by certain fixed rules, Charles attempts to impose a sense of order upon an essentially

disordered situation. In so doing, he repeats a pattern we have already seen exhibited on numerous occasions. For what is the transformation of emotional
turmoil into allegorical combat, and the metamorphosis
of natural scenery into a product of human creation, if
not the desire to impose order over random arrangement?

The game in all its varied forms was held in particular esteem by fifteenth-century French nobility.
First, it offered an escape from the unpleasant problems created by the rise of the bourgeois class and the
consequent erosion of aristocratic privilege. In the
ritualized battles fought on the chessboard and on the
tournament grounds the nobility found a reminiscence of
past glory dating to a time when its place in society
was assured by the vital military function it exercised. Reacting to the social anarchy resulting from
the period of the Hundred Years' War, the aristocracy
dedicated itself with an almost maniacal fervor to
devising ways of filling its existence with rules. For
each game, tournament, pageant, or new chivalric order
carried its own set of regulations, and these regulations had the effect of restoring a badly needed
measure of security.

Aside from producing an illusory feeling of order,
the game performed another important function. It provided a safe means of dramatizing, within carefully
controlled limits, potentially dangerous forces--aggres-
sion, fear, mistrust. Channelled into game activity,
these forces could be rendered momentarily harmless.
One might argue, therefore, that the seemingly frivolous pastimes of the period served a far more essential
purpose than is at first apparent.

Whatever psychological needs of the aristocracy may
have been fulfilled by games, they were above all else
an excellent means of filling idle time, a commodity
that Charles found increasingly abundant in the later
years of his life. Those pastimes requiring greater
mental than physical agility came to occupy large portions of his time. In addition to enabling him to keep
his wits sharp, they also allowed him the chance to
engage his favorite companions in conversation. Chess
remained one of his most beloved recreations. Warning
hypocrites and deceivers to use a little more subtlety
in constructing their schemes, he points out that good
chess players do not expose their pieces to attack.
The game they have chosen to play, he reminds them,

is not a simple one:

> Vostre besogne est trop ouverte,
> Ce n'est pas jeu d'entrejetteurs;
> > (2:401)

> (Your intention is too obvious;
> This is not a game for dice throwers;)

The metaphor of the game proves especially apt as a description of court society. Seen in this light, each gesture and turn of conversation represents a calculated attempt to manipulate the "opponent" according to a secret strategy.

In another poem he borrows terms from the billiard table. Complimenting René d'Anjou on his performance in a poetic duel between the two friends on the subject of love, Charles is quick to add that he himself has not done badly:

> Et j'ay mon billart bien tenu;
> > (2:298)

> (And I have handled my billiard cue well;)

The sexual innunendo needs no commentary. The duel may also pit the poet against an invisible adversary. Melancholy, for example, invites the poet's heart to engage in a fencing match:

> Ung baston qui point a deux boutz
> Porte, dont elle s'escremye.
> > (2:401)

> (A stick sharpened at both ends
> She carries, with which she fences.)

The contest, as Charles sees it, is an unequal one, and he attempts to persuade his heart to withdraw from certain defeat. Again the situation is constructed so as to allow avoidance of a confrontation, for the heart has the choice of accepting or declining the challenge of his opponent.

But if the poet can elect to disregard the provocations of Melancholy, there is one familiar antagonist whom he can never escape. Fortune, that one invincible adversary, engages her victim in the losing game of the hunt:

> Fortune, par ses faulz atrais,
> En pipant, a pris a la glus
> Mon cueur,....
>
> (2:378)

> (Fortune, with her deceiving charms,
> By peeping like a bird, caught
> My heart in glue....)

The ruse, an old trick for snaring birds, proves irresistible. Once a less crafty foe, relying on force more than wile, Fortune now resorts to more devious means of capturing her clever quarry.

The motif of the hunt surfaces again in the description of the heart's pursuit of Danger through the forest of Thought, a chase the poet likens to boar hunts of his past. Having cornered his prey, the heart unleashes his hounds of desire who are followed by the huntsman, Hope, spear in hand. The hunt, however, is essentially a one-sided sport, and the confrontation that most often appears in the rondeaux is one whose resolution remains in doubt. The meeting of male and female glances becomes a duel in which the eyes are

> Tous pres de combatre a oultrance.
>
> (2:338)

> (Completely ready to fight to the finish.)

It is not so much the result of the contest that is of interest, but the critical moment of maximum tension when the outcome hangs in balance.

Proverbs

Proverbial phrases in the Middle Ages enjoyed a popularity that they have never been able to fully recover. Collections of proverbs compiled during this period (about thirty of which exist in French) attest to a spoken language rich in means of figurative expression. Attracted by the poetic qualities of these time-worn phrases, Villon strung together several dozen into a single ballad. Working with fewer examples, Charles d'Orléans created a rondeau in similar fashion. Later writers--Marot, Rabelais, La Fontaine, Molière, and others--continued to exploit proverbial expressions for literary purposes before the vogue diminished in the eighteenth century. In a sampling of the adages found in Charles's rondeaux we find familiar sayings as well as some lost with time:

Onques feu ne fut sans fumee (2:309)
(Never was there smoke without fire)

Jeu qui trop dure ne vault rien (2:322)
(A game which lasts too long is no good)

Aprés chault temps vient vent de bise (2:322)
(After warm weather comes cold wind)

Le fer est chault, il le fault batre (2:347)
(The iron is hot, it must be struck)

Chose qui plaist est a demi vendue (2:361)
(A thing that pleases is half sold)

L'abit le moyne ne fait pas (2:362)
(The habit doesn't make the monk)

De fol juge brefve sentence (2:363)
(From a foolish judge a brief sentence)

Tel qu'on seme couvient cuillir (2:383)
(As one sows, so he reaps)

Polished by centuries of wear into the most concise possible form of expression, these ready-made verses are easily fitted into the appropriate context. When necessary, slight syntactical alterations prevent the phrase from jarring the rhythm of the poem, but the original figure of speech is always carefully preserved.

The use of proverbs belongs to a distinct register of Charles's late poetry, what might be called the "conversational register." Much less literary than the elevated discourse that characterizes most of his earlier and much of his later work, this contrasting style of expression follows the patterns of spoken rather than

written language. To cite only a few examples: "M'a-
pelez-vous cela jeu?" (2:404, "Are you telling me
that's a game?"), "Et de cela quoy?" (2:395, "And what
of it?"), "Alez vous ant, allez, alés" (2:320, "Away
with you, go, go"). Like these phrases, the proverbs
are taken from the popular speech that was to be heard
in the streets as well as in the castle of Blois. If
the highly refined language of the trouvères constituted Charles's legitimate poetic legacy, this fact did
not prevent him from dabbling with the earthy idiom of
peasants and peddlers. With their wealth of humor and
pithy wisdom the proverbs serve as an ideal "spice" for
his less serious poems.

In the colorful imagery of these proverbial expressions one may easily discern a certain element of folk
art. Their origins having long since been obscured,
proverbs were adopted as universal coinage in medieval
speech. Despite repeated handling, or maybe because of
it, the thought contained in a favorite adage did not
seem to lose its appeal. Perhaps it was its aura of
authenticity as well as its intrinsically poetic nature
that drew Charles d'Orléans and Villon to the proverb.
By including these and other samples of familiar
speech in literary genres formerly reserved for higher
modes of discourse, both poets, each in his own way,
helped to deflate the elitist pretensions of lyric
poetry.

Music

The aesthetic pursuits encouraged at Blois were not
limited to literary endeavors. From the ledger of expenditures it is known that the duke extended his generous patronage to musicians as well as poets. After
games, music ranked high as a popular pastime for the
late medieval nobility, and Charles was rarely far from
a source of such entertainment. He speaks, for instance, of being rudely awakened by the sound of a tam-
bourine summoning everyone to join in the May dance.
All festivals and processions offered a fine excuse, as
if one were needed, for an open air concert. Not all
music of the court was performed by professional musicians. The artistic activities of his young companions, according to Charles's description, were often
somewhat less than serious:

> L'un parle ou dort, et l'autre chante ou
>   crie,
> Les autres font balades ou rondeau.
>   (2:490)

> (One speaks or sleeps, and another sings or
>   yells,
> The others compose ballads or rondeaux.)

Whatever else Blois may have been, it clearly was not
an ascetic retreat for solemn and dedicated young poets
and musicians. Yet if this burst of creative energy
amuses Charles, his description contains barely a trace
of disparagement. His truly biting remarks are reserved for those engaged in less ingenuous pursuits.
We may be sure that a great deal of the artistic activity fostered in Blois was of a strictly amateurish nature. We may be equally certain that these efforts,
compensating for a lack of polish with a sincere desire
to please, were of valuable assistance to the duke in
his effort to elude melancholy and boredom.
    Referring to the writing of poetry or perhaps to the
act of speech itself, Charles encourages his readers to
verbalize their thoughts in musical form:

> Chantez ce que vous pensés
>   (2:310)

> (Sing what you're thinking).

A group of birds is a dancing chorus comprised

> De contres, deschants et teneurs
>   (2:309)

> (Of basses, descants, and tenors).

The natural harmony of birdsong, in a typical reversal,
becomes a human harmony of a trained choir. The trials
of the heart when portrayed in musical terms can hardly
be taken very seriously:

> Trop entré en la haulte gamme,
> Mon cuer, d'ut, ré, mi, fa, sol, la...
>   (2:473)

> (Gone too far up the high scale
> Of do, re, mi, fa, sol, la, my heart...)

In the remainder of the rondeau Charles proceeds to devise puns based on the names of the notes, such as <u>afola</u> ("frightened") and <u>hola</u> ("whoa").

A musician himself (a contemporary chronicler tells us that the duke sometimes performed on the harp), Charles possessed a remarkably sensitive ear. The musicality of his poetry, readily apparent throughout his work, is particularly discernible in the rondeaux. His standing today as a poet is based in large part (perhaps excessively) on his mastery of the mechanics of poetry writing. His verse, occasionally at the expense of intellectual content, moves with extraordinary fluidity. Working with alliteration and especially with assonance, Charles creates rich acoustical effects:

> Allez, allez, vieille nourrice
> (2:402)

> (Go, go, old nurse.)

> Se vous voulez m'amour avoir
> (2:421)

> (If you wish to have my love)

> Je suis ung de seulx, soulz la lune,
> Qu'elle plus a son vouloir dresse.
> (2:412)

> (I am one of those under the moon,
> Whom she [Fortune] most tames to her will.)

There is a subtle echoing quality to these verses similar to that found in many poems of Verlaine. Like the nineteenth-century poet, Charles enjoyed manipulating sounds in such a way as to create various musical effects. One way in which he enhances these effects is by modulating rhythm, as demonstrated in the following example:

> Puis ça, puis la,
> Et sus et jus,
> De plus en plus,
> Tout vient et va.
> (2:484)

> (Now here, now there,
> And up and down,
> More and more,
> All comes and goes.)

The brevity and bipartite division of each verse give a rapid pendular movement to the stanza, an impression further strengthened by the repetition of the vowel, consonant, or entire word in the second half of all four lines. Though full of musical qualities, the stanza is virtually devoid of any meaningful content. Communication at an intellectual level is obviously not the primary intent. These verses have to do with impression more than expression. A reading geared to content will therefore yield nothing but disappointment or frustration. A more fruitful approach would be to read the verses as an experiment—and a very successful one, at that—involving the use of sound and rhythm to produce a certain effect in the ear if not in the mind.

The musical element is not merely an ornamental feature of Charles's poetry. It is a vital and intrinsic part of his work. His art can only be fully appreciated when perceived sensorially as well as intellectually, for like Verlaine's, his poetry possesses a strong auditory appeal. It is inevitable then that even the most imaginative translation will read with a flatness that hardly does justice to the original. If his poems occasionally appear a little thin in content, we would do well to consider the poet's intent and judge the success of his effort accordingly.

Paul Valéry, in one of his many attempts to isolate the essence of poetry, compares poetry and prose with two types of human movement:

> Walking, like prose, always has a definite object. It is an act directed <u>toward</u> some object that we aim to reach....
>
> Dancing is quite different. It is, of course, a system of acts, but acts whose end is in themselves. It goes nowhere. Or if it pursues anything, it is

only an ideal object, a state, a delight.... (6)

The rondeaux of Charles d'Orléans, it might well be said, are as close to dancing as poetry can come. What may be true of all poetry is especially true of his. It is not enough that it be read. Only when read aloud does it take on its finished form.

Language Play

Fascinated not only by the subtleties of his native tongue but also by those of others, Charles mastered Latin and English well enough to produce correctly written and even fairly sophisticated verse in both languages. It is also probable that he spoke Italian with some degree of proficiency. One rondeau is composed of a surprisingly well blended mixture of French and a Lombard dialect. Latin phrases are to be found liberally sprinkled throughout the rondeaux, less a demonstration of erudition than another means of creating a comic effect. Foreign languages also enter his poetry in another way:

> Le trucheman de ma pensee,
> Qui parle maint divers langaige,
> M'a rapporté chose sauvaige
> Que je n'ay point acoustumee.
> (2:410)

> (The interpreter of my thought,
> Who speaks many different languages,
> Reported a strange thing to me
> Of which I have never heard.)

He goes on to explain that the interpreter first presented the story in its original language, then in French translation. The poet's heart still cannot comprehend the meaning of the communication, now called a "message," and asks the interpreter if he himself is not a foreigner. Thought by its very nature, we are reminded, remains a foreign language to the heart.

Experimentation with language does not always necessitate recourse to a non-native tongue. Charles's French, as we have seen, is not limited to the most highly cultivated strains of the language. He is not above using less refined varieties of speech when they

suit his purpose. Mocking the silly adult prattle
inspired by a baby's presence, he incorporates baby
talk into a rondeau:

> Quant n'ont assez fait dodo,
> Ces petiz enfanchonnés,
> Ils portent soubz leurs bonnés
> Visages plains de bobo.
>
> (2:387)

> (When these little children
> Haven't had enough nightie-night,
> They wear beneath their bonnets
> Faces full of boo-boos.*)

> *i.e., splotchy red marks

A father of three young children by the time he was
well over sixty, the duke had ample exposure to the
kind of talk he parodies here.

Whether it is a word taken from the lips of a
child's nurse, a foreign phrase dropped by an Italian
servant, a proverb overheard in the street, any linguistic ingredient is fit to be included in the poetic pot-
pourri of the rondeaux. Like a thrifty cook, Charles
throws away nothing that might be used. Snatches of
everyday conversation may be neatly integrated with
more literary language, or may even form the basis of
an entire poem, a dialogue, for example:

> D'Espoir? Il n'en est nouvelles.
> --Qui le dit? --Merencolie.
> --Elle ment. --Je le vous nye.
> --A! a! vous tenez ses querelles!
>
> (2:493)

> (About Hope? There's no news.
> --Who says so? --Melancholy.
> --She's lying. --I tell you she's not.
> --Aha! you're taking her side!)

The rest of the poem maintains the same lively cadence,
relying on a series of rapidly alternating responses to
create the impression of a spontaneous and even heated
exchange. From such examples of skillfully reconstructed specimens of conversational speech, it becomes evi-

dent that Charles possessed a true gift for language.
Had he tried his hand at farcical drama, an endeavor
considered beneath a man of noble birth, his perceptive
ear would undoubtedly have served him well.

Conclusion

In the final analysis, what is it about Charles's
rondeaux that gives them their special charm? The
answer, like the poetry itself, is elusive. One reader
might cite their gracious wit and subtle humor, another
their musical richness. Or it may be their highly
imaginative imagery that is found to be most appealing.
Whatever qualities have guaranteed their popularity,
these poems are one of the few literary products to
have survived five hundred years of changing tastes.
In fact, the rondeaux of Charles d'Orléans are virtually the only examples of this poetic genre read today by
the majority of students of French literature. Although the Middle French may occasionally pose problems
of comprehension, there is still a gracefulness of movement, a delicacy, a lightness of touch that will be apparent even to the uninitiated reader.

Chapter Eleven
Conclusion

The division of a writer's work into various periods, like the study of literature by century, is at best a rather arbitrary method of disposition, and one which should be used with great caution. Artistic temperaments tend to develop in patterns that defy simplistic categorization, and the attempt to separate an author's career into demarcated stages is almost certain to prove misleading. On the other hand, any critic faced with the task of surveying the entire output of a single writer must somehow attempt to facilitate the reader's understanding of at least the broadest outlines of that author's development.

In the case of Charles d'Orléans, the absence of a reliable chronology for most of the poems precludes the possibility of arranging them into more than two periods. The only accurate means of dating most of his poems is to place them either before or after his release from England in 1440. This distinction, minimal though it may seem, is a useful one. The date separating the two bodies of poetry happens to coincide with one of the most momentous events of the poet's life. Moreover, as the reader must be aware, certain peculiar characteristics sharply differentiate the post-exile verse from the work composed in England.

Verse Form

One of the most obvious differences between the two phases of Charles's poetry is related to form. While in England he preferred the more ample poetic forms: the ballad, the complainte, and the allegorical narrative. Once back in France, he concentrated on the rondeau. The transition from long to short form is not, however, as abrupt as it might seem. Toward the end of his stay in England Charles was already composing poems that were in effect rondeaux intended for musical accompaniment, i.e., the songs written for his English lady, and he continued to produce ballads after 1440, although with less frequency than in previous years. Still, the gravitation toward the rondeau is unmistakable. The reasons for this particular preference remain open to conjecture. It is probably safe to assume that he adopted the rondeau because he found it a more congenial poetic form. The question of form will be left open for a moment while we turn our attention to another aspect of Charles's poetry.

Orientation

It has been demonstrated that Charles's ballads written during captivity tend to be inwardly centered. With a proliferation of personified emotions and the development of the I/heart relationship, the poet explores his thoughts and feelings through his poetry. The exploration of the self by the self gives rise to a kind of paradox when subjected to the scrutiny of logic. In reply it might be said that any poetry operates with the right (even under the imperative, some would add) of illogicality. However, the interior world of Charles's ballads is not randomly arranged, but possesses an order, if not a logic, to which only its creator holds the key. This fact partially explains the difficulty of these poems.

Toward the end of the poet's years in England the conditions favoring the composition of introspective poetry seem to have disappeared, or at least to have lost a great deal of their influence over him. A new romance appeared, diverting much of the time and thought once devoted to more somber purposes. The contrast between the ballads and the songs—their form, tone, and themes—cannot fail to make a striking impression. From melancholy journeys through the labyrinth of the self, Charles now turned to outpourings of joy and praise, confessions of love, and insinuations of intimacy. Such a dramatic shift of focus required a fresh mode of expression, one at which the poet had not yet tried his hand. The new wine, in short, called for a new vessel.

Although it seems likely that the songs were composed after most of the pre-1440 ballads had been written, their uncertain date prevents any definitive location in the chronology of Charles's poetry. It has even been suggested that the lady whose death is commemorated in the nine poems previously discussed is the

same to whom the songs were addressed. The dating of
the rondeaux in relation to the early cycle of ballads,
on the other hand, poses no difficulty. The change of
generic preference appears, from all internal and external evidence, to coincide with a basic change of
psychological outlook. Avoiding the risky business of
extrapolating biographical observations from literary
evidence, let us limit ourselves to the poetry in question. The pre-1440 ballads are marked by pensiveness
and melancholy, the rondeaux by irony. The rondeaux
show a definite interest in the poet's immediate surroundings; in the ballads the poet is his own immediate surroundings. While the ballads define the self in
terms of its component parts, the rondeaux at least
begin to define it within the larger context of society.

Whether the romance described in the songs acted as
a catalyst in the evolution of the poetic perspective
is an interesting but unanswerable question. It does
seem logical, however, that of the two poetic genres
with which he was best acquainted, Charles should opt
for the one associated in his mind with an outward orientation. This conclusion is supported by the fact
that the ballads written after 1440, although employing
language and imagery clearly different from the earlier
ballads, basically retain the self-centered focus. The
orientation of Charles's poetry, it might then be said,
is a function of genre as well as chronology. It would
be wrong to assume that all introspection disappeared
from his verse after his return to France, but one has
only to compare the number of rondeaux to the number of
ballads composed after 1440 to appreciate the secondary
position to which this inwardly turned viewpoint has
been relegated.

Humor

Another characteristic of Charles's later verse is a
sensitivity to the inherent comedy of human society.
Hypocrisy, ambition, pride, all the motives so dear to
Molière and other comic playwrights, are variously
approached as subjects of ridicule or amused observation. Humor, moreover, is not limited to social
satire. The poet himself is a frequent target; his
age, infirmities, and eccentricities fuel numerous
self-parodies. Although Charles's sense of humor usual-

ly mainfests itself in decorous fashion, his poetry
also contains some rather explicit sexual innuendos,
proof that his humor runs the gamut from subtle to
ribald.

While occasional traces of humor may be found in his
earlier poetry, the verse composed in England is, understandably, rather sober by comparison. This fact along
with a failure to distinguish adequately between his
two literary periods and an insistence on taking all of
his verse at face value has led to a common misconcep-
tion. According to the opinion of many critics,
Charles was continually plagued by depression and bitterness, a kind of romantic ennui which is evidenced
especially in his later work. The editors of a fairly
recent survey of French poetry present this typical
assessment: "In the days of his old age, the poet sings
a strange weariness of life and cultivates the contrast
between the sadness of his heart and the joy of renew-
al" (1). Such an appraisal completely disregards the
major role of humor in Charles's poetry after 1440.
True, he complains, reminisces, and laments, but the
sincerity of his protest is almost constantly undercut
by a strong sense of irony. It is this very irony, in
fact, that endows his verse with so much of its wit,
vigor, and charm. To neglect this aspect of his work
does serious discredit to the poet, and deprives the
poetry of what is perhaps its most vital and noteworthy
quality.

Language

One of the most significant changes separating the
two phases of Charles d'Orléans's poetic career is the
movement toward diversification of language, a trend
visible in the later ballads as well as in the rondeaux. With the introduction of proverbial expressions, an abundance of conversational remarks, terminol-
ogies borrowed from medicine, theology, and a variety
of recreational activities, the poetic vocabulary becomes vastly enriched. This infusion of new forms of
language coincides with a revitalization of imagery.
As the poet explores various types of metaphorical representation, a wealth of new images, sometimes con-
trived, often highly imaginative, appears. The later
poetry, on the whole, is more colorful and more pictori-
al than the earlier work.

The enrichment of the linguistic medium can also be
correlated with another aspect of Charles's post-exile
verse. The earlier poetry is written primarily in a
single tone, which we might call, for lack of a better
term, the "courtly register." As a relatively inexperienced poet, Charles evidently felt most comfortable
working within the same framework used by the great
lyric poets of the past. Introspective meditation, confessions of love, emotional conflicts, all lend themselves well to the abstract language prescribed by
courtly tradition. After his repatriation, however, a
new register appears alongside of the old one. This
added mode of discourse is characterized by its tendency toward graphic language, and also by less formalized
and occasionally earthy expression. By mixing the two
registers the poet achieves a variety of interesting
effects. All of these stylistic features--increased
irony, lexical flexibility, the addition of a new
poetic voice--attest to the continuing development and
eventual maturation of Charles's talent.

The Doulx Seigneur and the Povre Escolier

The "gentle lord" and the "poor schoolboy": so
Villon refers to Charles d'Orléans and himself in his
long poem praising Charles's recently born daughter. A
comparison of these two poets offers more than a point
of incidental interest. The differences between their
biographical backgrounds needs no elaboration. Their
poetry, however, shares more than might be expected.
Of the dozens of French poets who wrote during the fifteenth century, they are the only two who are widely
known and read today. Their sustained popularity may
be explained in large part by their individualism, a
word more often associated with Villon than Charles
d'Orléans, but applicable in varying degrees to both
poets.
Time, specifically its measurement through the aging
process, is a primary theme in the work of both men.
Villon presents himself at the outset of the Testament (half in jest perhaps, but even his jests deserve
to be taken seriously) as an old man:

> I mourn the days of my youth
> When more than most I had my fling
> Until age came upon me. (2)

As we have seen, Charles already shows an interest in the passage of time in the Songe en complainte (he was then forty-three; Villon wrote the Testament at thirty), and continues to show an increasing preoccupation with the subject in the rondeaux and later ballads. It should be reiterated that this awareness of the transience of human existence reflects a common line of medieval thought. Villon and Charles d'Orléans, however, demonstrate a particular sensitivity to the phenomenon of aging which sets them apart from their contemporaries. Each poet personalizes the theme in a manner to which the modern reader can readily respond.

Most of the other similarities, each deserving far more elaboration than can be provided here, have already been suggested in the course of this study, and will simply be listed in summary form for the purpose of synthesis. Both poets display a remarkable sense of humor which permeates their work (in Charles's case, the poetry composed after his repatriation) and opens it to various levels of reading. Another important shared characteristic is a certain receptivity to language and subject matter traditionally excluded from lyric verse. The humorous bent of this poetry and the willingness of its creators to experiment with language go hand in hand with a sense of playfulness, an evident desire to amuse. Both men enjoy puncturing courtly illusions with barbs of cynicism, realism, and satire. Most important, both develop an original poetic personality, one whose precise relation to the poet's actual character cannot be accurately determined, but which nonetheless conveys some notion of each man's unique outlook on life.

Charles d'Orléans in the History of French Poetry

Charles d'Orléans is often described as the last of the great courtly poets. There is some truth in this assessment. His earlier ballads carry on the lyric tradition of Gace Brulé, Thibaut de Champagne, and other trouvères, a tradition passed on to the fifteenth century via Guillaume de Machaut and other less prominent poets. Charles is also remembered for his contribution as a patron of poets. The importance of Blois as a forum for poetic activity, a workshop for producing images, to paraphrase Daniel Poirion, certainly

deserves to be recognized. Because of the long history
of Paris as the artistic as well as the civil capital
of France, it is often forgotten that literary creation
has not always revolved aroung this city. Charles's
contribution to the history of French poetry, however,
goes beyond his well-established reputation as a courtly poet and patron of the art.

His influence on succeeding generations of poets
would perhaps be easier to measure if the genres he mastered had survived well into the sixteenth century.
Clément Marot, as it happened, was the last important
poet to use the ballad and the rondeau. The other
major poets of the sixteenth century flatly rejected
pre-Renaissance poetry, both in form and content, and
turned to what they considered to be more sophisticated
vehicles such as the sonnet and the Pindaric ode.
Their break with the past encompassed, they believed,
not only the adoption of new genres but a whole new
mode of lyric expression. While the impact of Petrarch-
ism, Neoplatonism, and the other new intellectual currents of the period should not be minimized, neither
should we lose sight of the debt of the Renaissance
poets to their immediate predecessors. The great medieval poets, Charles d'Orléans as much as any other,
bequeathed to their successors high poetic standards,
models of exceedingly rigorous discipline, and a feeling for the musical possibilities of the French language.

Granted, French poetry underwent far-reaching
changes in the course of the sixteenth century. Still,
as medieval and Renaissance scholars alike have
stressed in recent years, the transition from one period to the other was not nearly as abrupt as it was once
believed. To position Charles d'Orléans just outside
the great bronze doors of the Renaissance may help
editors of historical anthologies tie their excerpts
into neat packages, but it does little justice to the
continuity of French poetry.

Charles's most important contribution to the fifteenth, sixteenth, and later centuries of French poetry
is one for which he shares credit with Villon,
Deschamps, and a handful of other poets. Like them,
he was instrumental in effecting a gradual personaliza-
tion of the lyric. A crucial distinction must be made
here. The traditional lyric was personal, but not per-
sonalized. It allowed the listener/reader access to

the poet's thoughts and feelings, but rarely conveyed any information about the person himself and the facets of his personality that made him a unique individual. The audience expected to enter the poet's "I," to find in it a universality of experience with which it could identify. Gradually the poetic "I," particularly its distinguishing characteristics, and its relation to the poet, became a point of interest in itself. Curiously, Charles's work is a microcosm of this evolving poetic pattern. The first stage tends to portray the interior world, the poet striving to capture the immediacy of his mental and emotional experiences. With the second stage another dimension is added to his work, namely, perceptions of the natural and human world surrounding him and a new perspective of himself as a part of this world.

Through these changes, and especially through the detachment that made them possible, Charles d'Orléans created a distinctive poetic personality that is today attracting increasing attention and admiration. As a military leader, a ruler, a statesman, Charles d'Orléans achieved little by which to be remembered. As a poet, he is assured of a secure position in French letters, and one which is likely to gain stature in years to come.

Notes and References

Chapter One

1. There is no precise English equivalent for
fin'amors. "Pure love" is one translation. "Perfect
love" is another.
2. For a brief and informative introduction to the
troubadours see Henri Irénée Marrou's Les Troubadours (Paris: Seuil, 1961).
3. Bernart de Ventadorn from Anthology of Troubadour Lyric Poetry, ed. and trans. by Alan R. Press
(Austin: Univ. of Texas, 1971), p. 77.
4. For a succinct and penetrating analysis of the
effects of war and plague on the late medieval mentality, J. Huizinga's The Waning of the Middle Ages remains unsurpassed. A lengthy but highly readable account of French life toward the end of the fourteenth
century is provided by Barbara Tuchman's A Distant Mirror (New York: Knopf, 1978).
5. The term bourgeois appears in Old French as
early as the twelfth century, but was used throughout
the Middle Ages in a much more restricted sense than today, typically applied to any inhabitant of a bourg
("town"). The influence of this new social order upon
fourteenth and fifteenth-century French literature has
yet to be fully explored.
6. A copy of Froissart's Dit Royal was purchased
by Louis d'Orléans in 1393, a year before Charles's
birth.
7. Daniel Poirion, Le Poète et le prince (Paris, 1965), p. 232.

Chapter Two

1. In the appendix to his edition of Charles's
poetry Champion gives the text of a work entitled "Le
Livre contre tout peché" ["The book against all
sins"], a charmingly naive poem of 149 lines covering
each of the seven deadly sins. The author identifies

himself in the poem, but part of the name is mysterious-
ly scratched out, leaving "Je, nommé
d'Orléans." The name "Charles" can be read beneath
the deletion. The author, according to the poem, was
ten years old at the time he wrote this piece.
    2. Although no reference to Deschamps appears in
Charles's poetry, it is almost certain that the two
were personally acquainted, for the older poet was one
of the family's most frequent guests. Valentina pro-
fessed a great admiration for Deschamps, and the respect appears to have been mutual.
    3. Both men were earnest advocates of peace and
dedicated themselves to achieving this goal. While
Charles's efforts were generally treated with indifference by his countrymen, Suffolk later became the scape-
goat of a reactionary faction of the English nobility
and was accused, among other things, of conspiring with
Charles d'Orléans. In 1450 he was assassinated on
orders from his enemies.
    4. The exact date and nature of Bonne's death have
never been accurately determined. Information concerning her life after 1415 is, in fact, practically nonex-
istent.
    5. "Madame, vu ce que vous avez fait pour ma de-
livrance, je me rends votre prisonnier."
    6. Champion's edition of Charles's poetry is based
on a dozen manuscripts, most of which date to the second half of the fifteenth century. By far the most complete and reliable of these sources is the one designated as O (Bibliothèque nationale, fr. 25458) which
contains many poems in Charles's own hand and served as
his "guest book" at Blois. For facsimiles and a de-
tailed study of this text see Champion's Le manuscrit
autographe des poésies de Charles d'Orléans (Paris,
1907).
    7. Charles d'Orléans, Poésies, Pierre Cham-
pion, ed., 2 vols. (Paris, 1924-1927), 2:316. Here-
after references cited in text in parentheses are to
this edition. All translations are my own.

Chapter Three

    1. To avoid unnecessary awkwardness, I have fol-
lowed the example of John Fox and others in using the

English term "ballad" in lieu of ballade.
2. Machaut was one of the last poets to score his ballads. Although a few composers such as Dufay occasionally wrote musical accompaniments, the genre was virtually divorced from music by the end of the fourteenth century.
3. The envoi, originally considered an optional appendage to the main body of the ballad, was adopted into standard usage well before the earliest known codification of the ballad form appeared in Jean Molinet's Art et science de rhetorique in 1493.
4. Louange des dames, ed. by Nigel Wilkins (New York: Harper and Row, 1972), p. 59.
5. Reason, having been incorporated into the poetic "I," rarely appears in personified form—a total of only three times in the exile ballads.
6. Champion convincingly argues that the ballads are addressed to Bonne, although this opinion is not universally accepted by Charles's critics and biographers. Failing to find a single piece of contradictory evidence, I accept his hypothesis as a reasonable assumption. In the interest of biographical accuracy, however, and following Charles's discretion, I have refrained from making any dogmatic statement concerning the woman's identity, and will refer to her simply as the poet's "lady" or "mistress" (the latter term to be taken in its archaic rather than its modern sense).
7.
> Tresmalade, mon testament
> J'ay mis en escript doloreux.
> (1:96)

> (Gravely ill, my testament
> I have put into sorrowful writing.)

8. The closest analogy in medieval French literature to Charles's letter-ballads is the series of lyric pieces inserted into Guillaume de Machaut's narrative, Le Voir Dit [The true story]. Machaut claims these poems to be actual letters exchanged between the aging poet and his young mistress. Recent scholarship, critically examining the alleged correspondence, has cast serious doubt on its authenticity.
9. The earliest attestation of public knowledge of

these ballads comes from Martin Le Franc in 1442.
    10. Champion dates all nine poems between 1434 and
1436.

Chapter Five

    1. Champion proposes 1414 as the date of composi-
tion, but cites no supporting evidence.
    2. For further resemblances between early lyric
poetry and the medieval legal system, see R. Howard
Bloch's Medieval French Literature and Law (Berkeley:
University of California, 1977).

Chapter Six

    1. In a treatise on famous lovers, Le Livre du
Cuer d'Amours espris, Charles's intimate acquaintance,
René d'Anjou, refers to a romance his friend pursued
while in England:

        Car prins fuz des Anglois et mené en seruaige
        Et tant y demouray qu'en aprins le langaige
        Par lequel fus acoint de dame belle et sage
        Et d'elle si espris qu'a Amours fis hommaige.

        (For he was captured by the English and led
            into bondage
        And stayed there so long that he learned the
            language
        By which he made the acquaintance of a wise
            and lovely lady,
        And was so taken by her that he swore homage
            to Love.)

Chapter Seven

    1. The only existing copy of the manuscript is
housed in the British Museum (Harleian 682).
    2. Robert Steele, The English Poems of Charles
d'Orléans (Oxford: Oxford University Press, 1941-
46).
    3. Champion refutes this opinion, pointing out
that the omission of the poets' names would be an act
of carelessness totally uncharacteristic of Charles
d'Orléans.
    4. Raphael Holinshed, Chronicles of England,

Scotland and Ireland (edition of London: J. Johnson, 1808), vol. 3, p. 196.

5. John Fox attempts in his article, "Charles d'Orléans, poète anglais?" <u>Romania</u> 86 (1965):433-62, to discredit the theory of a translation. In spite of his enthusiastic endorsement of Steele's hypothesis, he does not include a section on the English poetry in his book on Charles d'Orléans.

Chapter Eight

1. See Note 6, Chapter Two.
2. The friendship of Charles and René is proved by more than the exchange of poems; the two also traded gifts of horses, silver goblets, and handsome weapons.
3. About Fredet, as in the case of many other contributors to the album, we know practically nothing. Champion states that Charles first made his acquaintance in Tours in 1444, and that Fredet later made several trips to Blois. His name is one of the most frequent to appear in the album where he left a <u>complainte</u> as well as numerous rondeaux.
4. Poirion, <u>Le poète et le prince</u>, p. 181.

Chapter Nine

1. See rondeau 97 (Champion) for a reworking of these verses.

Chapter Ten

1. Matisse, incidentally, produced a very limited edition of selected poetry by Charles d'Orléans, writing out each poem by hand, and including numerous illustrations. One of these depicts the duke as envisioned by the artist.
2. Rondeaux composed before the sixteenth century are sometimes referred to as <u>rondels</u>, the older form of the term. A good deal of confusion surrounds the use of these two terms. Although some literary manuals attempt to draw a distinction between the two, no clear consensus exists. In referring to Charles's poems as rondeaux I am following the nomenclature established by Champion and used by the poet himself.
3. For additional observations on the problem of the <u>rentrement</u> see O. Jodogne's perceptive remarks in

"Le rondeau du xve siècle mal compris," cited in my
bibliography.

4. I have omitted Champion's comma after bou-
derie since this interpretation allows an ambiguity
which, in my opinion, distorts the intended meaning of
the text.

5. La Rochefoucauld, Maximes (Paris: Garnier,
1967), p. 11.

6. Paul Valéry, The Art of Poetry, trans.
Denise Folliot (New York: Random House, 1958), pp.
206-7.

Chapter Eleven

1. Jean-Paul Chauveau and Jean-Charles Payen, La
poésie des origines à 1715 (Paris: Colin, 1968), p.
46.

2. The Poems of François Villon, trans. Galway
Kinnel (Boston: Houghton Mifflin, 1977), p. 37:

Je plains le temps de ma jeunesse
Ouquel j'ay plus qu'autre gallé
Jusques a l'entree de viellesse (v. 169-71).

Selected Bibliography

PRIMARY SOURCES

CHAMPION, PIERRE, ed. Charles d'Orléans, Poésies. 2 vols. Classiques français du moyen âge. Paris: Honoré Champion, 1924-1927. By far the most reliable and most available edition of the complete works.

PURCELL, SALLY, trans. The Poems of Charles d'Orléans. Cheshire, England: Carcanet Press, 1973. Careful translation of selected poems. Many of most important pieces omitted.

SECONDARY SOURCES

CHAMPION, PIERRE. Charles d'Orléans. Paris: Honoré Champion, 1908. The definitive biography, meticulously researched.

_____. Le manuscrit autographe des poésies de Charles d'Orléans. Paris: Honoré Champion, 1907. Describes the manuscript on which Champion's edition is largely based. Contains facsimiles of poems in Charles's hand.

CHOFFEL, JACQUES. Le Duc Charles d'Orléans: Chronique d'un prince des fleurs de lys. Paris: Debresse, 1968. Brief biography focusing on Charles's political activities.

CIGADA, SERGIO. L'Opera poetica di Charles d'Orléans. Milan: Vita a pensiero, 1960. A sensitive and sensible interpretation by one of the poet's most highly respected critics.

DARBY, GEORGE O. "Observations on the Chronology of Charles d'Orléans rondeaux." Romantic Review 34 (1943):3-17. Challenges Champion's dating of several rondeaux.

FOX, JOHN. "Charles d'Orléans, poète anglais?" Romania 86 (1965):433-62. Makes a persuasive case for attributing disputed English poems to the French poet.

_____. The Lyric Poetry of Charles d'Orléans.
Oxford: Clarendon, 1969. A useful introduction to
Charles's poetry. Contains good chapters on liter-
ary background and versification.

FRANÇON, MARCEL. "Les refrains des rondeaux de
Charles d'Orléans." Modern Philology 39 (1942):
259-63. Questions Champion's editing of refrains in
the rondeaux.

_____. "Note sur les rondeaux et les chansons de
Charles d'Orléans." Studi Francesi 11 (1967):87-
97. Brief remarks on the problem of the rentrement.

GOODRICH, NORMA L. Charles d'Orléans: A Study of
Themes in His French and in His English Poetry.
Geneva: Droz, 1967. Defends Charles's authorship
of disputed English poetry by establishing existence
of similar thematic patterns.

HARRISON, ANN TUKEY. Charles d'Orléans and the Allegorical Mode. North Carolina Studies in the Romance Languages and Literatures, No. 150. Chapel
Hill: University of North Carolina Department of Romance Languages, 1975. Solid scholarly treatment of
French and English poetry within the context of
courtly allegory.

JODOGNE, OMER. "Le rondeau du quinzième siècle mal
compris" in Mélanges de langue et littératures
médiévales offerta à Pierre Le Gentil, pp. 399-
408. Paris: S.E.D.E.S. et C.D.U., 1973. Demonstrates the structural complexities of a seemingly
simple form.

MACLEOD, ENID. Charles d'Orléans, Prince and Poet.
London: Chatto and Windus, 1962. Well written and
entertaining. Excellent biographical introduction.

NEWMAN, KAREN. "The Mind's Castle: Containment in the
Poetry of Charles d'Orléans." Romance Philology
33 (1980):317-28. Advocates multileveled interpretation of poetry with emphasis on religious coloring.

PLANCHE, ALICE. Charles d'Orléans ou à la recherche
d'un langage. Paris: Honoré Champion, 1975. Ex-
haustive study of imagery tending toward description
more than analysis. Includes interesting comparison
of Charles d'Orléans and Mallarmé.

POIRION, DANIEL. "Charles d'Orléans" in Le moyen
âge. Littérature française, Vol. 2, pp. 211-219.
Cogent appraisal of Charles's most important poetic
contributions.

_____. "Création poétique et composition romanesque dans les premiers poèmes de Charles d'Orléans." Revue des sciences humaines 90 (1958):185-211. Discredits various attempts to interpret Charles's poetry in light of biographical data, emphasizing role of courtly tradition.

_____. Le lexique de Charles d'Orléans dans les Ballades. Geneva: Droz, 1967. A valuable reference tool.

_____. "La nef de l'espérance: symbole et allégorie chez Charles d'Orléans" in Mélanges de langue et littérature du moyen âge et de la renaissance offerts à Jean Frappier. Geneva: Droz, 1970. Classification and perceptive analysis of ship and boat images.

_____. Le poète et le prince. Paris: Presses Universitaires de France, 1965. An indispensable introduction to French lyric poetry of the fourteenth and fifteenth centuries.

SEATON, MARY E. Studies in Villon, Vaillant and Charles d'Orléans. Oxford: Blackwell, 1957. An imaginative search for acrostics with interesting but often farfetched results.

STAROBINSKY, JEAN. "L'encre de la mélancolie." Nouvelle revue française 123 (1963):410-23. Brilliant study of mélancolie in the rondeaux focusing on liquid images associated with the term.

STEVENSON, ROBERT L. "Charles d'Orléans" in Familiar Studies of Men and Books, pp. 201-42. New York: Scribner's, 1895. A highly readable, sometimes overgeneralized account of the poet's life as revealed through his writing.

ZUMTHOR, PAUL. "Charles d'Orléans et le langage de l'allégorie" in Lange, texte, énigme, pp. 197-213. Paris: Seuil, 1975. Linguistic analysis by a major medievalist and structuralist critic.

Index

Adam de la Halle, 5, 116
Amboise, 22
Aristotle, 13
Ars Nova, 9
Art de dictier, 116
Asti, 20, 89
Azincourt, 6, 15, 43

Ballad form, 9, 23-24,
    152
Baude, Henri, 23
Baudelaire, Charles, 37,
    113
Bernart de Ventadorn, 2
Blois, 20, 85, 88, 89,
    94, 95, 105, 118, 129,
    139, 140, 151
Bonne d'Armagnac, 14,
    17, 18, 19, 38, 40,
    46, 75
Brulé, Gace, 5, 151
Bubonic plague, 6-7

Caillau, Jehan, 21, 102
Canzo d'amors, 3-5,
    11, 79, 80
Champion, Pierre, 117
Chanson d'amour, 5
Chanson de Roland, 5,
    59
Charlemagne, 59
Charles VI, 14, 15
Charles VII, 20, 89
Charles de Nevers, 88,
    118
Charles d'Orléans:
    childhood and adoles-
cence, 13-15; exile in
England, 15-19; later
years, 19-22

POETRY:
Ballads, 18, 23-53,
    76, 83, 96-114, 115,
    116, 119, 128, 146,
    147, 148
Carols, 18
Complaintes, 54-62,
    84, 146
Retinue d'amours,
    18, 63-65
Rondeaux, 21-22, 75,
    83, 88, 96, 100,
    115-45, 146, 147,
    148
Songs, 18, 19, 75-83,
    147
Songe en complainte,
    18, 65-74, 96

Chartier, Alain, 23
Chastellain, Georges,
    92, 94
Chaucer, 23
Chrétien de Troyes, 74
Christine de Pisan, 9-
    10, 23
Cicero, 13
Cigada, Sergio, 86
Conon de Béthune, 5

Damien, Benoist, 92,
    112

Danse macabre, 7
Deschamps, Eustache, 10-
  11, 14, 23, 39, 116,
  152
dizain, 24
Dover, 43, 44, 54
Du Bellay, Joachim, 61
Dufay, Guillaume, 94

Fin'amors, 2, 11
Fox, John, 85
Fredet, 93
Froissart, Jean, 6, 9,
  23

Garbet, Nicolas, 13
Gille des Ormes, 92, 112
Goodrich, Norma, 86
Grands rhétoriqueurs,
  94
Guillaume d'Aquitaine, 2
Guillaume de Lorris, 64,
  108
Guillaume de Machaut, 8-
  9, 10, 24, 116, 151

Holinshed, Raphael, 85
huitain, 24
Huizinga, Johan, 103
Hundred Years' War, 5-6,
  8, 12, 89, 135

Jean d'Alençon, 88
Jean de Bourbon, 88
Jean II de Bourbon, 90,
  91
Jean de Meung, 8, 10
Jean-sans-Peur, 13, 14,
  15
Jeanne d'Arc, 43, 59
Jeux-partis, 74

La Fontaine, Jean de,
  23, 138
Lai, 9
Langue d'oc, 2

La Rochefoucauld,
  François duc de, 123-
  24, 125
Le Gout, Etienne, 93
Loire, 13, 108
Louis XII, 22
Louis d'Orléans, 9, 10,
  13, 14

Marie de Clèves, 20
Marot, Clément, 23,
  116, 138, 152
Matisse, Henri, 115
Meschinot, Jean, 92, 94
Molière, Jean-Baptiste
  Poquelin, 138, 148
Muset, Colin, 8, 10, 118
Musset, Alfred de, 116

Neoplatonism, 152

Olivier de la Marche, 92
Orléans, 59, 108, 118
Ovid, 13

Parnassian movement, 23
Perceval le gallois, 13
Petrarch, 76, 117, 152
Philippe de Bourgogne,
  20, 88
Pindaric ode, 152
Pléiade, 23
Poirion, Daniel, 94, 151
Proverbs, 137-39

Rabelais, François, 138
René d'Anjou, 85, 88,
  92, 118, 136
Rimbaud, Arthur, 108
Roman de la Rose, 8,
  10, 13, 64, 108
Romantic poets, 119
Rondeau form, 9, 23,
  115-17, 152
Ronsard, Pierre, 61, 76
Rudel, Jaufré, 2

Rutebeuf, 8, 10

Saint Augustine, 13
Saint Bernard, 13
Saint Louis, 59
Sonnet, 117, 152
Steele, Robert, 84, 85,
   86

Thibaut de Champagne, 5,
   151
Thomas d'Angleterre,
   74
Touraine, 118
Tours, 118
Tristan, 24
Troubadours, 1-5, 79,
   80, 81, 103, 119
Trouveres, 74, 103,
   119, 139, 151

Valentine's day, 26, 51,
   64
Valéry, Paul, 142-43
Venus, 85, 86
Verlaine, Paul, 141, 142
Villon, François, 1,
   21, 23, 28, 69, 92,
   95, 106, 124, 137,
   139, 150-51, 152
Virelai, 9, 23
Visconti, Valentina, 13,
   14
Virgil, 13
Voiture, Vincent, 23,
   116
Voltaire, François-
   Marie Arouet de, 116

William de la Pole, 16-
   17

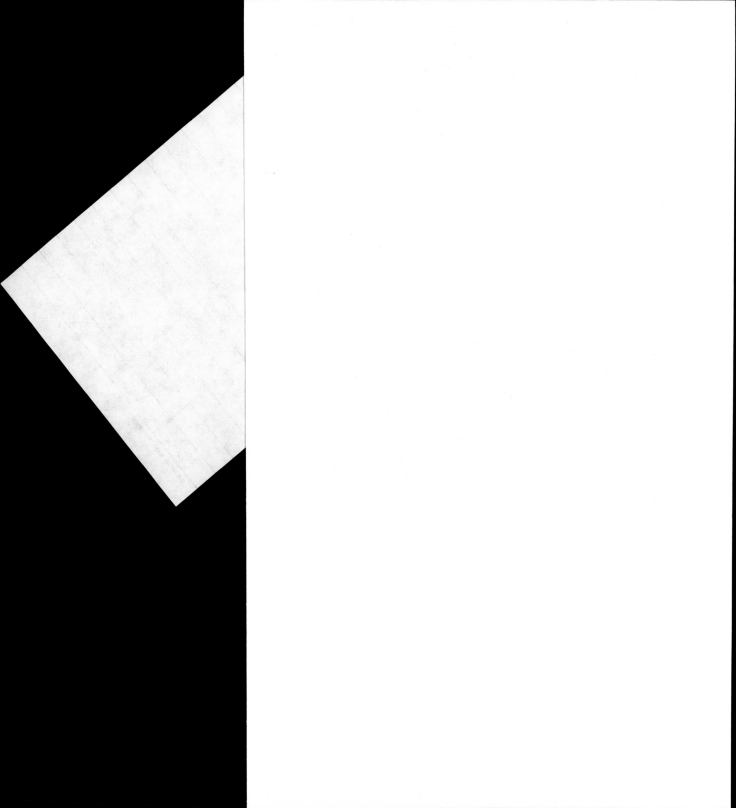

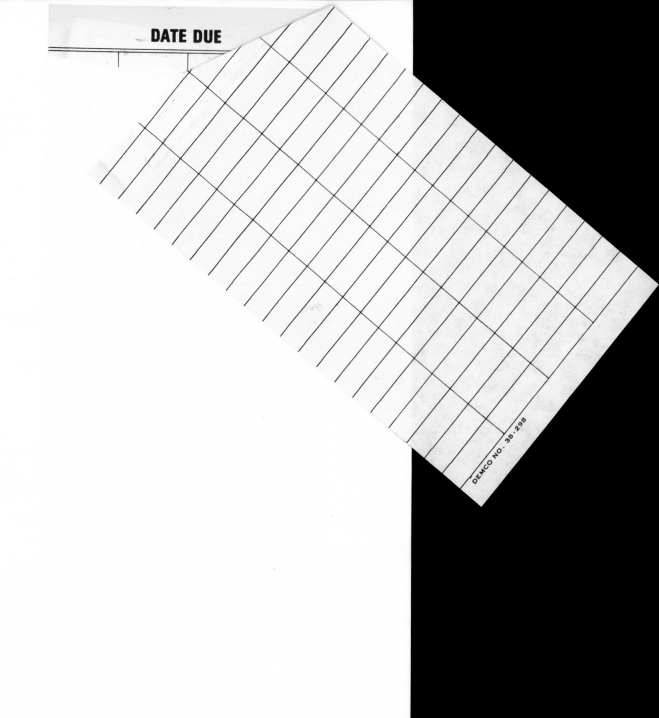

DATE DUE